MONEY MATTERS FOR TEENS

BUDGETING, INVESTING AND PERSONAL
FINANCE FOR TEENS ON THE ROAD TO RICHES

WISE YOUNG WALLETS

Dedicated to Taig, a dear friend, without whom this book would not have been possible.

CONTENTS

INTRODUCTION

The fuel that keeps the wheels of our world turning is money; it gives products and services a certain worth and enables the billions of daily transactions that support the modern economy. Without it, the transfer of wealth would, simply, stop.

This crucial function has been provided by money for thousands of years. Before its creation, people traded their items for other people's necessities in a process known as *bartering*. For simple transactions, bartering would do, but not when the goods sold had different worth or their equivalent were not accessible. Now, in contrast, money is universally acknowledged and has a uniform (consistent) value: this gives us a reference point as to whether goods and services are relatively expensive or cheap. It is a straightforward idea, but it has evolved into a complicated state over time.

Whoa! Stop right there.

This is a book for teens, right?

The financial markets are, indeed, complex, and for the high-flying investors in the corporate world, what happens there might make as much sense to you as, say, astrophysics or neurology formulations embedded in calculus.

In other words, we'll stick to the basics; which is what this book is all about.

People claim "money doesn't make you happy"; I don't believe this to be entirely true. To me, money is *freedom*, and while I may still be on my journey to financial freedom, I know I've got the determination, motivation and knowledge to get there. For me, money allows me to *choose* to do what makes me happy.

As famed American poet EE Cummings once said: "It takes courage to grow up and become who you really are."

Indeed. And for all of you who are embarking on understanding finances, which is necessary to make your way in the world, this book will provide a comprehensive head start!

Picture this: with the right financial skills, you can fund your dream education without drowning in student loans, embark on epic journeys that take your breath away, invest in your wildest passions and ideas and build a rock-solid foundation for your future. Imagine being able to buy whatever you want, whenever you want - where you're not having to think about squeezing every penny, rather, you have the tools and knowledge to thrive in a world where money becomes your trusted ally, not a daunting foe.

So, gear up for an exhilarating journey towards financial empowerment, where every dollar you save and invest today opens doors to a future teeming with vibrant opportunities and a life beyond your wildest dreams! Let's dive in and uncover the dazzling possibilities that await you on *your* path to financial freedom.

Finance, however, is just the beginning, as this book aims to propel you towards realizing your deepest ambitions, with strategies for teen entrepreneurism and landing your first job. It's dedicated to giving you the know-how to succeed - that's where the courage bit comes in.

It's not easy. It's darn hard. But come on, you're the class of 2023 and you're out to prove to the world that you have the knowledge and the determination to make it!

So, first things first - fearless finance, let's go!

1

BUILDING A SOLID FINANCIAL FOUNDATION

"When money realizes that it is in good hands, it wants to stay and multiply in those hands."

— IDOWU KOYENIKAN

$

D oes the idea of delivering newspapers appeal to you?

In my early teenage years, it certainly did to me, as that was another couple of bucks in my pocket. I couldn't wait to add to the money slowly accumulating in my piggy bank, which was kept securely locked; only I had the key.

Bit by bit. I was putting it together.

I made a sign with the words "Jake's Bank" and stuck it on the front.

My parents were proud of me and it was a great way to start earning money and exercising simultaneously!

If you're looking for somewhere to start, I urge you to think about it.

On the other side of town, Erin was diligently collecting her babysitting money. She had opened a savings account and deposited the money straight in; the very same account she still uses six years later. As for me, I eventually put my money into a savings account as well. Similarly, one I still use to this day. For both, it is a reminder of good beginnings.

And the piggy bank with "Jake's Bank" proudly plastered on it?

In my apartment, it has pride of place atop my bookshelf.

We may have been young, but we were already going places!

Fiscal Foundations

If you're in your teens and on the cusp of adulthood, did you have similar beginnings with your start in the money world? Did you have inner stirrings that what you did with your money was of the utmost importance, or was it something to spend as fast as possible?

With finance not taught early in schools, if at all, it's understandable that the answer to this question often gives a divided response.

While many had a similar beginning to myself and Erin's, many were reckless with money; disinterest in financial matters can play a part in the outlook of many a teenager or young adult.

Furthermore, growing up in a disorderly or chaotic environment where monetary knowledge isn't given any importance, aside from the worry that rent will be paid, unfortunately doesn't often offer the basis for a solid financial future. There are circumstances, though, where a desire to acquire financial literacy can come through sheer will and determination; these changes are certainly cause for celebration.

However, for those whose parents or guardians have established a financial plan for you early on - great stuff! Don't let it go to waste.

While perhaps, at first, overwhelming, empowering yourself with financial know-how can be for everyone. The more thorough the background, the more likely you will become an expert in no time - anyone can become one, it's all up to you!

UNDERSTANDING THE VALUE OF MONEY

This book aims to answer many of the big financial questions you may have, including how to invest for the future, how to maximize your income, how financial markets work and how governments control money. Discover essential knowledge on everything from compound interest to credit cards and learn how to manage your own money, from payments to pensions. Make use of the handy glossary at the back of the book if there are financial terms you haven't come across yet.

What is Money and How is it Used?

Did you know the first forms of money were agricultural merchandise, such as grains and livestock? Today, money comprises worldwide currencies that financial institutions manage and standardize; each has a relative worth with respect to others (this is represented by the Foreign Exchange Rate).

Goods and services have a specific value and money allows us to trade them as we need. Money is relied on not only to allow for such transactions, but to also assist economic financial growth.

You may have come across the term *legal tender*; this, by legal definition, refers to bank notes and coins. However nowadays, with the introduction of wireless technology, you'll be well aware that most people chose to pay via credit or debit card, and more advanced still by contactless means. It is entirely up to a vendor (salesperson) to decide what 'tender' to accept; it's simply a matter of discretion. Although having said that, they may lose considerable business if they suddenly chose to exclusively accept Monopoly money and baseball cards.

What is Inflation?

Simply put, inflation is the rate of increase in prices over a certain period of time. It is typically a broad measure, calculated using the Consumer Price Index (CPI). When general price levels rise, your money buys fewer goods and services, for example rent, groceries, health care, insurance, education and recreation. Inflation correlates to a reduction in the *purchasing power* of money. In the same way, when prices fall over time, this is *deflation*.

What are the Different Types of Money?

Commodity Money

In a barter system, specific resources are used as exchanges, for example: gold coins, beads, shells, pearls, stones, tea, sugar and metals; the value of this kind of money comes from the amount assigned to it. This *tender* has inherent (built-in) value, and is only limited by its scarcity (how much of it there is).

Whenever any commodity is used for exchange purposes, it essentially becomes money. There are certain types of commodities used for this purpose, including several precious metals like gold, silver, copper, etc. Elsewhere in the world, seashells, tobacco, cocoa and other commodities were used as money. As mentioned earlier, it is at the vendors discretion to decide the medium of exchange.

Fiat Money

The word *fiat* means "command of the sovereign." Fiat currency is the kind of money that does not have an underlying or intrinsic value and cannot be used as a valuable resource, as per the example commodities above - it is not backed by tangible assets.

Previously, the Gold Standard was the monetary system that based the value of a Government's currency against a fixed quantity of gold. This in turn led to states in the US holding large quantities of gold reserves. However, this was finally abandoned in the 1970's due to the constraints it imposed on Governmental systems.

Today, Fiat money is the foundation of all monetary policies. It is any global currently used as legal tender by its Government. Examples of fiat money are the British Pound and the US Dollar.

Fiduciary Money

Fiduciary money is a slightly more complex concept, as it is a system of exchange where there is a *promise of money* to be given at a later date, rather than exchanged immediately. For example, a $1000 check is a promise of money, however the paper itself is worthless until it is cashed in and converted to *fiat* money within a bank account.

Commercial Bank Money

Commercial money represents loans generated from global financial institutions, such as banks lending consumers mortgages. It is a vital part of the economy, as it facilities the buying and selling of assets.

BUDGETING BASICS: SPEND, SAVE AND INVEST

If you're new to budgeting, it is important to understand what a budget is and how it allows you to expertly manage your money.

A budget is a financial strategy that details your income and records how much you spend, for example monthly, quarterly or annually. Reviewing your financial situation and examining your needs and wants is a vital first step in planning your budget, but beware, noting areas where you are overspending can be a jarring experience!

Creating a budget and not deviating from it will help you realize your short and long-term financial goals. This is a continuous exercise and you should always recalculate if you have a financial windfall or setback so it reflects your current situation.

It is first important to have a basic understanding of common phrases and keywords you are likely to find in budgeting plans and templates.

Budgeting Terminology

Total monthly income is earned from your job or other resources, including investment dividends, pensions, Social Security benefits and rental income (we'll get into these later). Your total income before any taxes or loan payments is also called your **gross income**.

Disposable income (also referred to as disposable personal income, or DPI) is the money remaining after subtracting your taxes, also called your **net income** (taxes are mandatory payments to the Government that are taken from the wages of workers and the profits of businesses or added to the prices of some goods, services and activities).

Your disposable income is the money you are supposed to live on every month and is the basis for your monthly budget and annual spending. You can use your disposable income to calculate how much you can spend. On a broad scale, DPI is constantly evaluated as one of the key economic indicators used to gauge the overall state of the economy.

When financial advisors counsel individuals, they ask them to estimate their expenses, dividing the necessary and non-negotiable, like mortgage and car payments, from those that are fluid, like entertainment costs. This is the difference between fixed and flexible expenses.

Fixed expenses do not change, such as rent payments. As a general budgeting rule, ideally 50% of your net income should cover your required costs; for instance, if this is $2000, you should allocate $1000 to your needs.

Flexible expenses can vary from month to month and are optional purchases that can be altered or removed without a significant change to your lifestyle. Economists often use the term "consumer discretionary spending" to describe flexible expenses.

Such costs can be further classified as they often contain flexible components that, when scrutinised, can help you adhere to your budget, such as choosing a more affordable television or music subscription, eating out at fewer restaurants and taking less vacations.

To begin your budget, add your **fixed costs** to your **flexible expenses** to reach your **total outgoings**. This is the total amount of money you spend over one month.

The next step is to make a monthly budget using a budget worksheet. If you are out of line with your budget, you may either be spending beyond your means or your budget needs to be more flexible. Review and readjust your budget accordingly until you find a plan that works for you. Some example monthly templates are included at the end of this chapter to help get you started.

How Do You Budget All Your Expenses?

At the start of the month, plan how you will spend your money that month. Calculate what you think you will earn and spend.

At the end of the month, see if your planning was correct.

Use the information to help you plan the following month's budget. Consider fixed and flexible expenses plus the following:

- Building an Education Fund - You can save money for future college expenditures through a 529 college savings plan, a state-sponsored investment plan.
- Emergency Fund – Save money to cover your bills for three to six months in the event of an unexpected circumstance, such as the loss of your job.
- Retirement Fund
- Saving for a Goal
- Travel Budgeting

Budgeting rules 50/30/20

This rule states that you should spend up to half of your after-tax income on needs and obligations that you need to meet. The remaining half should be split between 20% on savings and debt repayment and 30% on everything else you want.

50%: Needs

Needs are those bills you must pay and that are necessary for survival. Half of your after-tax income should be all that you need to meet your needs and obligations. If you spend more on your needs, you will have to either minimize your wants or downsize your lifestyle, perhaps to a smaller home or a more modest car. Carpooling or taking public transportation to work is the answer, and you could try cooking at home more often. Examples of "needs" include but aren't limited to:

- Rent or mortgage payments
- Car payments
- Groceries
- Insurance and health care
- Minimum debt payments
- Utilities

As a teenager, it's unlikely you'll have many, if any, of these outgoing costs. But it's great to know what you'll face as you move through life. For now, you might delegate all the funds in this category, into savings or wants (I recommend saving!).

· · ·

30%: Wants

Wants are everything you buy that is optional. Anything in the "wants" bucket is optional if you examine it carefully. You can exercise at home instead of going to the gym, cook instead of eating out, or watch sports on TV instead of going to the game.

20%: Savings

Finally, allow 20% of your net (after-tax) income to savings and investments. You should aim to have at least three months of emergency savings in your kitty if you lose your job or an unforeseen event occurs. After that, focus on building for your retirement (even though it seems a million years away) and meeting other financial goals. Examples of savings could include:

- Creating an emergency fund
- Making IRA (Individual Retirement Account) contributions to a mutual fund account
- Investing in the stock market
- Saving to buy physical property for long-term holding
- Saving for your education

Example of the 50/30/20 Budget Rule

You've recently graduated from college and started your first full-time job. You want to build good financial habits from the start and have heard about the 50/30/20 budget rule. Eager to manage finances effectively, you set up a 50/30/20 budget.

To understand personal spending patterns, you start scrutinizing expenses over a month. You use a budgeting app that allocates expenses automatically into needs, wants, and savings. You calculate monthly after-tax income, which amounts to $3,500. This will be the basis for issuing a budget according to the 50/30/20 rule.

After analyzing tracked expenses, you realize that essential expenses like rent, utilities, groceries, transportation, and student loan payments amount to approximately $1,750 per month. You allocate exactly 50% of your income, which is $1,750, to meet these needs and then allot the remaining $1,050 (30%) to various items and $700 (20%) monthly to retirement and savings. (To calculate the percentage of your income, multiply by 0.2 for 20% and 0.3 for 30%.) You set up an automatic transfer from a checking account to a savings account on payday.

Six months later, you are promoted. Because your income has changed, each budget amount is re-evaluated. In addition, there is a review of the budget, and necessary adjustments are made. You realize that transportation expenses are higher than expected, so begin to start carpooling with a colleague to reduce costs.

You remain disciplined and consistent with the budgeting practice, prioritize financial health and regularly evaluate progress toward goals. As the career progresses, continual adjustments are made to the budget to accommodate changes in income and priorities.

This is a formula for success!

Signs you are spending too much money

Here are seven red flags that indicate you're spending more than you can afford and tips for correcting this.

1. Your budget is based on your salary or hourly rate

If you budget your money based on your pretax number rather than the after-tax amount, you're overestimating how much you can afford to spend. Use an online calculator to find your take-home pay and go from there. For example, you earn $12 an hour before tax, but the actual number you take home is more like $10 an hour, depending on a lot of factors.

. . .

2. Your expenses exceed your income

When you evaluate your monthly fixed and variable expenses – from rent to food to your gym membership – this amount should not exceed your monthly income. If it does and you don't cut back on your budget, you may end up in debt.

3. You have a negative net worth

When your expenses exceed your income for too long, you may have a negative net worth – where what you owe is greater than what you own in assets. This is a common scenario with most young adults with student debt. On the other hand, you will have a positive net worth if you don't owe anything. To find out your net worth, minus what you owe (student debt, for example) from your assets (things you own such as a car).

4. You consistently owe money on your credit card

Using a credit card for all or most of your purchases is perfectly fine as long as you can pay off the balance in full every month. If you don't, or you make the minimum due, the remaining balance will begin to accumulate interest and grow exponentially.

Consider consolidating your debt with a personal loan or a 0% balance transfer card.

Balance transfer credit cards, which allow you to transfer debt from other sources and pay as low as 0% interest for an introductory period, and debt consolidation loans, which are unsecured personal loans used to pay off debt, are two of the most popular ways to help pay down debt and save money along the way.

When it comes to saving money, paying off debts every month is the most significant money drain. Debt takes away your money! So, you should pay off that loan. The debt snowball method is the fastest way to pay off debt. This is where you pay off your bills, starting with the smallest and going up to the biggest. Sounds scary, doesn't it? Don't worry, it's not about the numbers. It's about changing how people act. Once you have more money to spend, you can finally put it toward your savings goals.

5. Your rent or mortgage exceeds 30% of after-tax income

You are probably not renting yet, but this is good to know: an accurate way to determine if you're overspending on housing is to limit your monthly expenses to 30 percent of your after-tax income. This can be difficult in a high-cost-of-living city, but it's a good point to aim for. Use an online calculator to calculate your take-home pay, multiply that by 30% (0.3) and divide by 12 to get your target number.

Suppose your take-home pay is $25,000 a year. $25,000 x 0.3 = $7,500 which is the annual amount. $7,500 / 12 = $625 which gives your monthly amount.

6. You buy things to keep up with or impress your friends

Social media exacerbates (makes worse) the "Keeping up with the Joneses/Chans/Kardashians" affliction that affects many of us. You don't know the financial situation of each of your friends, and merely surmising that you can afford something because they can – or worse, you're trying to impress them – would not be sustainable.

7. You aren't saving at all

There are a lot of helpful apps that you can use to examine where your money is going every month and which can help you choose what to cut back on or eliminate. Or better still, meet with a financial planner who can help map out a strategy for short-term and long-term savings goals.

If you're not saving anything, you're not getting any closer to your goals.

You have more control over your money than you may realize.

TEEN TV.

LISA – BUDGETS AND EPIC COOKING FAILS!

Lisa, a friend of mine, has been trying to maintain her extravagant lifestyle while sticking to a strict budget, with hilarious results. She begins by making a comprehensive budget with separate categories for fixed costs like rent, electricity, and groceries. But things get interesting when Lisa starts trying to figure out how much money she needs to spend on fun activities.

She resolves to be resourceful rather than simply reducing her discretionary spending. She begins by participating in low-cost or no-cost pursuits such as visiting nearby parks, hosting game evenings with friends, and attending community functions. This way, she can still have a good time without breaking the bank.

Lisa constantly searches for bargains to get the most out of her money. She subscribes to emails from local establishments, uses money-saving applications, and watches social media sites for discounts. This allows her to save money while still participating in her preferred activities.

Lisa's juggling act isn't without its bumps, though. Many comical incidents occur. For instance, she tries to save money by cooking at home more often but has such epic cooking fails that she resorts to takeout.

She also makes a horrendous mess of her kitchen when she tries to save money by repairing things herself. For a whole week, she had little access to the kitchen. She spent a lot of time at the nearby café that week, and the tab quickly added up. Not only that, but she needed more than a plumber to put the room back together!

Lisa is determined, though, to make her budget work without losing too much of her happiness despite the occasional setbacks she may have. She gains insight into the importance of setting financial priorities, being resourceful in the face of adversity, and seeing the funny side of things.

The intelligent teen's quest to find a happy medium between her extravagant wants and her limited resources is a humorous journey full of unexpected turns and surprises. She learns the best way to balance having fun and being responsible with her money through trial and error.

You go, girl!

Delayed Gratification

In today's regular practice of one-click purchases and immediately accessible information, instant gratification is seen as the norm. This "constantly available" world, with smartphones and Wi-Fi, reinforces the ideology that you must get whatever you want immediately.

But instant gratification can mess you up. You realize that constantly working on impulse control is a vital life skill. Delayed gratification will get you there faster when it comes to achieving your goals.

The truth is, it's not realistic or healthy to get everything you want, much less get it immediately. Instant gratification is a source of frustration – it promotes false expectations. By learning to employ delayed gratification, you buy time to think carefully and learn from your failures. But what is delayed gratification? And how can you acquire this crucial skill?

As we mature, the "I want it now" desire is halted by the "reality" principle, or the ability to consider risks versus rewards, by which we're able to delay fulfilment instead of making a faulty decision – especially if the latter reward is greater than what we'd get immediately. This is delayed gratification.

Delay the gratification of buying something you don't need and earn the long-term reward of having more savings.

You may not get instant returns when you invest, but the delayed gratification is even more significant as you build your money.

Here's your plan:

1. Start small

To train your brain toward delayed gratification, start small. Create a goal so easy you can't refuse it. Suppose you wait three minutes before eating dessert. Next time, improve by one percent – or in this case, you can improve by 33% and wait for four minutes. Incremental progress lets you achieve confidence with each small goal you achieve.

2. Make rules

You can also use delayed gratification as a "rule" for certain areas of your life where you may lack self-control. If you're a shopaholic, make it a rule to wait three days – or a week – to buy that jacket you saw online. Or make a rule that if you've spent more than five minutes debating a purchase, you don't go ahead with that purchase.

3. Practice gratitude

Reminding yourself of all you have is a great way to train your brain to accept delayed gratification. When you think of the stocked wardrobe you're already lucky enough to have or the perfectly good car you own, you realize you don't need that new stuff you've been aching to buy. Instead of being disappointed you're having a salad for lunch rather than a burger, be grateful that you have food to nourish your body. Delayed gratification comes naturally when you practice gratitude.

4. Remind yourself of your goals

What is delayed gratification for, if not the ability to reach your biggest goals and dreams? You're rejecting an unnecessary purchase to save for a home or retirement and eating more inexpensively and healthily. Keep a picture of your goals on your phone – you can even set it as your wallpaper – to remind yourself what you're working toward. It will make delayed gratification that much easier.

How can delayed gratification help you achieve your long-term financial goals?

There are a few things you can do financially that will ensure you reach your long-term goals:

Save enough money before purchasing to avoid credit card debt or a personal loan. When you incur a debt, make sure you can pay it off quickly.

If you invest in a term deposit (a fixed-term investment that includes the deposit of money into an account at a financial institution, with an interest payment at the end of the term), don't give in to the urge to take it out before the maturity date. Savor the wait so you don't lose the interest you've earned.

If you're saving up a deposit to buy a property, try to save up for a bigger deposit so you'll potentially borrow less in the future.

Reinvest any dividends you might get from your shares to increase your total number of shares. Doing this could result in greater returns in the long term.

Exercising delayed gratification can help you take control of many aspects of your life, so why not start with your finances?

Use a savings calculator to determine how much you must put aside each payday to reach your financial goals.

SETTING SMART FINANCIAL GOALS

Setting financial goals is a vital first step toward realizing your vision for your future financial situation. But it's easy to make the mistake of setting overly general goals like getting out of debt or saving enough for retirement. Goals like this can be easier to accomplish if you break them down using the SMART goal strategy.

The SMART acronym stands for Specific, Measurable, Achievable, Realistic and Timely. Read how to set your own SMART financial goals and raise your odds of success.

1. Set <u>Specific</u> Goals

Make your financial goals distinct so you clearly understand what you want to achieve. The more well-defined your goal is, the easier it will be to plan how to get there.

For example, start with the general idea that you want to save more money or that you want to start investing in retirement. These are good starting points, but meeting goals with a clear target is easier.

How much do you want to save from each paycheck? How much money do you want to invest for retirement?

Make these goals more specific by defining them further: "I want to automatically transfer a portion of each paycheck into a high-yield savings account" or "I want to save for retirement by automatically investing a portion of each paycheck into my 401(k)."

Specific financial goals will help you understand precisely what you want to achieve, how you'll know you're on track, how you'll do it and when you plan to achieve your goal. In short, specific financial goals are more precise, more motivating, and easier to achieve.

2. <u>Measure</u> Your Progress

Make your financial goal measurable by finding ways to quantify your progress.

Regarding saving, such as for an emergency fund, you can make your goal quantifiable by allowing how much and how often you'll save: "I'll automatically transfer $50 from each biweekly paycheck into a high-yield savings account." That way, you'll know what to do to achieve your goal and see if you're on track.

If you have a retirement goal of putting some of your income into a Roth IRA (a special individual retirement account in which you pay taxes on contributions, and then all future withdrawals are tax-free), make this goal measurable by highlighting your contribution amount: "I'll defer 15% of each paycheck into a Roth IRA." Periodically check your progress to see if you are on track.

3. Make Your Goals <u>Achievable</u>

To make your financial goal achievable, identify what steps you'll need to take to bring your plan within reach.

For example, when investing for retirement, one of the best ways to make your investing goal a reality is to set up automatic contributions. When you automatically pay yourself first by sending money into your retirement account, you'll avoid the temptation to spend the money elsewhere.

Also, you can make your investing goal achievable by ensuring you can live on what's left of your pay after you deduct your contributions. Start by tracking your spending and creating a budget.

You can also make your financial goals more achievable by cutting unnecessary spending and looking for ways to increase your income.

4. Keep Goals <u>Realistic</u>

Create financial goals that are realistic for you. Setting an unrealistic financial plan can help you extend yourself, but ensure you set goals within reach.

For example, if you plan to get married in two years, having a savings goal for a $100,000 luxury wedding would be difficult, if not impossible, for an average earner to accomplish.

Instead, plan your goal around what is affordable. For example, you could lower your budget to a more attainable goal of $28,000, the average cost of a wedding ceremony and reception in 2021. Or you could push your wedding out for a few years to make saving for a larger wedding more realistic.

5. Include a <u>Timeline</u> to Complete Your Goal

Most goals require deadlines. That's why you should have a timeline when you set financial goals.

Suppose your goal is to save $1 million by retirement. In that case, you can break that goal into smaller achievable goals with deadlines. You might aim to save $7,000 for retirement by the end of this year. Alternatively, you could rearrange your retirement goal by focusing on the shorter-term goal of saving three times your salary by age 40.

When it comes to reducing high-interest debt, assigning yourself deadlines for how much of your balance you'll have paid down can help you stay on track and create a realistic plan.

If you have $20,000 in credit card debt, you should make paying it down as fast as is realistically possible a top goal. To make a SMART debt payoff plan, you could earmark a deadline for when you'll be out of debt, such as within two or three years. With a smaller balance, you might aim to be debt-free within one year.

If you have a high credit score, consider combining SMART goal setting with savvy credit product strategies to reduce debt more efficiently. Transferring your balance to a card with a lengthy 0% introductory APR (Annual Percentage Rate) period could save you a lot of money on interest, and it provides you with a deadline.

If your introductory APR period ends in 18 months, you'll need to commit to making monthly payments to eliminate your debt in full before the introductory period ends. You could accomplish the same thing with a personal loan, with a fixed term and monthly installments acting as built-in timelines.

KEY TAKEAWAYS

- **Understand the value of money – how it works and the different types.**
- **Budgeting Basics – how to expertly manage your money.**
- **The budgeting rule 50/30/20 – the master plan of managing needs, wants, and savings.**
- **The power of delayed gratification – the amazing results of not giving in to instant gratification.**
- **Setting SMART financial goals – knowing what you want to achieve will give you a head start.**

COMING UP

In Chapter 2, we will elaborate on the importance of savings and emergency funds and highlight the basics of banking. You'll also learn how to manage debts and use a credit card correctly!

BUDGET PLANNER

INCOME

DATE	DESCRIPTION	AMOUNT

EXPENSES

DATE	DESCRIPTION	AMOUNT

TOTAL INCOME	
TOTAL EXPENSES	
REMAINING BALANCE	

BUDGET PLANNER

Incomings

Date	Description	Amount
Total		

Fixed Expenses

Date	Description	Amount
Total		

Other Expenses

Date	Description	Amount
Total		

Recap

	Goal	Actual	Difference
Earned			
Spent			
Saved			

50/30/20 BUDGET PLANNER

Projected Monthly Income

Income 1	
Extra Income	
Total Monthly Income	

Actual Monthly Income

Income 1	
Extra Income	
Total Monthly Income	

Needs 50%

Description	Projected Cost	Actual Cost
Subtotal		

Wants 30%

Description	Projected Cost	Actual Cost
Subtotal		

Savings 20%

Description	Projected Cost	Actual Cost
Subtotal		

Total Monthly Income	
Total Monthly Expenses	
Difference	

2

UNLEASHING THE POWER OF PERSONAL FINANCE

"Do not save what is left after spending but spend what is left after saving."

— WARREN BUFFETT

THE IMPORTANCE OF SAVING AND EMERGENCY FUNDS

Over half of Americans have failed to keep pace with their retirement savings, and 17% of Americans aren't saving anything, according to Bankrate.

Rarely is the value of saving money challenged. One of the primary (and often repeated) pieces of financial advice is that you have to save, though many of us don't do it.

CNBC found that 58% of Americans live from paycheck to paycheck, meaning that the loss of their job or a large unexpected cost could be catastrophic, possibly even leaving them homeless. Families are getting increasingly stressed because of rising prices due to inflation and the possibility of a recession.

. . .

More than just understanding that you should save money is required when making the appropriate financial decisions.

Saving money involves self-control and some degree of sacrifice, which could involve a massive change in your persona.

Suppose you want to persist with a savings strategy throughout your working career. In that case, understanding the benefits of saving money is vital. Ensure you understand these essential explanations of why you should start saving money immediately if you need assistance in comprehending their significance:

Saving can set you free.

Suppose you have yet to find a specific purpose in mind for the money. In that case, allocating an amount from your income to a savings account may be difficult. Why save money when you can merely go on a spending spree? Even if you are still deciding what you're saving for, you will get an idea of what you want to save for in the process, which is just one of the many benefits of saving money. The options are bountiful: a new car, a vacation, your education and so on. Additionally, having something saved up for emergencies and unforeseen costs is essential.

"It has nothing to do with the money and everything to do with awarding yourself flexibility and more choice in your life," says Eric Roberge, CFP® and founder of a financial planning business that focuses on offering financial guidance to people in their 30s.

"When you have available money in the bank, you are free to spend without stress," he claims. If you're unsure of why you should save money, consider the freedom it will give you to pursue your interests rather than being forced to remain in a certain condition or circumstance because you live solely from paycheck to paycheck, making it very hard to save.

You can set aside a certain monthly amount based on what you can afford to save after things like retirement savings and emergency fund contributions are accounted for.

Financial security.

"I love saving money because it means financial security," says Kara Perez, the founder of a business that promotes financial literacy with a slant on empowering women by awarding them the knowledge and resources they need to achieve their financial objectives.

Essentially, having money makes life easier, according to Perez. "I save because I don't want to be caught in a financial emergency, and I want to live the same lifestyle I do now."

You can take calculated risks.

When you save money, you build cash reserves, permitting you to take measured chances with less stress. With minimal reserves, it will be more difficult to follow specific interests. Consider the process of launching a business. You'll need financial backing to get your small business up and running.

"Saving gives you the freedom to live life on your terms," explains Matt Becker, CFP® and founder of a financial planning practice aimed at new parents.

"When I lost my job three years ago, my wife and I took advantage of the opportunity to launch the businesses we'd been planning," Becker explains. "We could only make that decision because of the years we'd been building our savings."

Consider the steps below if you are new to saving or need help sticking to your savings goal.

. . .

Keep track of your spending: If you find it hard to save regularly, try being aware and keeping track of your monthly expenses. This will give you a clear picture of what is happening with your money. You can then identify non-essential products and aim to save more money by avoiding them.

Make a savings budget: Creating a monthly budget is desirable. You can plan to target savings and set spending restrictions at the beginning of each month. This allows you to zone in on what is essential, minimize the likelihood of overspending, and will enable you to save as planned.

Limit your credit card use: Credit cards may provide a short sense of relief, but the high interest rates will have a detrimental effect. It is advantageous to reduce your debt and limit credit card expenditures to keep your savings intact and build all the while. You may not have a credit card yet, but there are options for younger people with no credit history. These cards have a minimal limit but build your credit score quickly. It's a great way to learn about the world of credit cards.

Invest in long-term financial tools: It is vital to see your savings keep growing when you save. Investing in a long-term plan can provide numerous additional advantages. These plans offer a lucrative rate of return, permitting your money to retain its value and outperform inflation. The savings or endowment plan is devised along these lines.

A recent Northwestern Mutual insurance company study also found that saving is associated with a better mood. The study found that those who are "planners" and do things like setting goals and going the extra mile (for instance, saving money) to reach those goals feel happier and better about their lives than those who don't.

Similarly, the Consumer Federation of America found a strong link between having spending and saving strategies and having emergency funds on hand. Those with a spending plan with goals were much more likely to have saved money for emergencies than those without a plan, especially low-income persons.

Emergency Funds

We've all had "out of the blue" unanticipated financial problems, such as a car accident, an unexpected medical bill, a broken appliance, a loss of income, or even a broken cell phone. These unexpected expenses, whether large or small, seem to happen at the worst possible times.

Setting up specific savings or emergency funds is one of the most important things you can do for your protection, and it's one of the first steps you can take to begin saving. By allocating money for these unanticipated expenses, even if it's a modest amount, you can recover quicker and get back on your feet to meet your larger savings goals.

Your circumstances determine the amount you should have in an emergency savings fund. Consider the most typical types of unexpected expenses you've encountered and how much they cost. This can help you allocate how much you need to put into the fund.

Putting money aside can be challenging if you live paycheck to paycheck or get paid a different amount each week or month. However, even a tiny sum might bring the financial security you need.

It may be tempting to utilize the funds to take a trip, place a deposit on a new home or vehicle, fund an extravagant wedding, or any other major expense that arises, so you should make a list of approved expenses for your money.

Ensure that they are true emergencies, such as living expenses and groceries when you are unemployed, unexpected medical problems, home repairs due to a natural disaster or fire, unplanned veterinarian bills, vehicle repairs, or surprise tax bills.

The entire purpose of an emergency fund is to keep you from having to go into debt or scrounge for money at the last minute. You want to be able to concentrate on the situation rather than finding funds to cover it.

Saving money is a learned skill.

Building a savings account of any size is easier when you can consistently save money. It's one of the quickest ways to see it grow. Suppose you aren't in the habit of saving. In that case, there are a few essential elements to developing and maintaining a savings habit:

Make a plan. Having a clear financial goal will help you stay on track. Creating an emergency fund may be the attainable objective that keeps you grounded, especially when you're just starting. Use a savings planning calculator to determine how long it will take to attain your goal based on how much and how frequently you can save.

Make a system for consistent contributions. There are numerous ways to save money, and one of the easiest is to set up automatic recurring transfers. You might also save a certain amount of money each day, week, or during the payday period. Aim for a certain amount, and if you can afford to do more occasionally, your savings will increase even faster.

Monitor your progress regularly. Make a habit of checking your savings account regularly. Whether it's an automatic notification of your account balance or having a running amount of your contributions (keep this online), tracking your success can provide motivation to keep going.

. . .

Celebrate your accomplishments. If you're sticking to your savings plan, take advantage of the chance to celebrate your success when you reach your goal. Once you've met your financial objectives, create a new one.

BANKING BASICS – Checking, Savings and Credit

What is a savings account?

A savings account is a deposit account that pays interest at a bank or other financial institution. Though these accounts typically yield only a low-interest rate, their safety and reliability make them great for storing funds for short-term requirements.

Savings accounts may have some restrictions on how often you can withdraw funds. Still, they generally provide exceptional adaptability that's perfect for building an emergency fund, saving for a short-term goal like buying a vehicle or going on vacation, or simply depositing surplus cash from your checking account to earn extra interest.

Because of their safety, liquidity, and interest-earning potential, savings accounts are a suitable place to put money for future use instead of daily drawing dollars. These accounts are ideal for storing emergency money or saving for short-term goals such as a vacation or home repair.

What is interest?

Interest is the expense of borrowing money or the cost of lending money. Interest is most commonly shown as an annual percentage of the borrowed amount. This is known as the loan's interest rate.

For example, when you deposit money in a high-yield savings account, a bank will give you interest. The bank rewards you for keeping and investing your money in other transactions. Alternatively, suppose you borrow money for a major expense. In that case, the lender will charge you interest on top of the borrowed amount.

When you borrow money, you must repay the base amount (the principal) plus the loan's interest to your lender. These loans occur in a variety of forms. Credit cards, vehicle loans, mortgages, personal loans, and other forms of debt accrue interest. It is critical to understand how the interest terms and repayment criteria operate.

Banks often utilize various principles to determine your interest rate when lending, including your credit score and debt-to-income ratio. It also depends on the type of loan, such as a credit card or a mortgage. Also, commercial lenders typically charge a separate fee for creating a loan with a consumer.

Say you wish to apply to your bank for a $5,000 loan. To determine the interest rate it will charge you, your bank must calculate how much interest it spends to obtain the funds it will lend to you (say, 4%). The bank will also incur loan service fees and overheads, which will be factored into your interest rate (say, 2%). Of course, the bank must account for default risk and profit (say, an additional 2%). To cover these fees, your loan may have an interest rate of approximately 8%, which is $400. This means when you repay the principal amount, you must also add the interest, making you liable to pay back a total of $5400.

What is a checking account?

A checking account is a type of deposit account that allows you to make withdrawals, deposits, and fund transfers easily. Checking accounts, also known as demand accounts or trans-actional accounts, can be accessed by cheques, automated teller machines (ATMs), and electronic debits, among other ways. They are frequently used to accumulate money for short-term costs.

Opening a checking account with a bank or credit union is usually simple. You can apply online or in person at a bank and generally can acquire a checking account immediately.

The institution will require essential personal information such as your Social Security number and identity.

You can then deposit into the account with cash or a check. (Some checking accounts have a minimum deposit amount.) You will usually be given a debit card, which you can use to deposit and withdraw funds as needed via ATMs, checks, or in-person transactions. You can also use your bank account to transfer funds or pay bills online.

The Federal Deposit Insurance Corp (FDIC) guarantees funds in a checking account at a bank up to $250,000 per individual depositor at each insured bank. That implies your money will be secure if you have less than that amount and you or the bank defaults (got bankrupt). Any money above the FDIC limit is in danger of being protected.

Similarly, suppose you open a checking account at a credit union. In that case, your funds will be protected by the National Credit Union Association in the same way.

Checking accounts are classified for their intended use. Businesses, for example, use a commercial checking account. The company's managers and workers will be able to utilize the account for business expenses.

Several banks offer student checking accounts with benefits such as no maintenance or minimum balance fees; helping students learn how to manage their finances.

Services for Checking Accounts

Direct Deposits & Debits

Direct deposit and direct debit are two common financial transactions used in banking.

A *direct deposit* allows a corporation, such as your employer, to electronically transfer money into your bank account, such as your paycheck. You will then have immediate access to funds.

A *direct debit* is set up by the bank account holder and allows the electronic transfer of money to a recipient, for example setting up regular payments for a cell phone bill.

Wire Transfer

A wire transfer is an electronic funds transfer that moves money from one account to another. It enables money to be transmitted securely without the need for cash exchange. Wire transfers are usually used for one-off payments, whereas direct debits are commonly used for regular payments such as a salary.

ATMs

ATMs provide instant access to cash. They are machines found at bank branches or other public places such as malls, airports or convenience stores. Ensure you understand the costs your bank charges for accessing ATMs outside of its network, for example, when abroad.

What is credit?

Bank credit is the amount of money available from a banking organization in the form of loans to a business or individual. Bank credit covers the entire sum of money an individual or corporation can borrow from a bank or any other financial institution.

The bank credit of a borrower is calculated by the ability to repay loans and the total amount of credit available to lend by the banking institution. Car loans, personal loans and mortgages are examples of bank credit.

Now this is where it gets interesting; the loans banks are able to give out are actually derived through deposits made by clients into checking and savings accounts! This means when you deposit your $200 birthday check, banks use this money for their own purposes, for example loans and investments. But don't fear, your money will always be readily available to withdraw from the bank, just not from the pot you thought!

Credit is a contract between banks and borrowers; a bank effectively trusts borrowers to repay the principal sum as well as interest at a later date by issuing credit. The creditworthiness of a person determines whether or not they are authorized for credit and how much credit they receive.

NAVIGATING THE WORLD OF CREDIT CARDS

A credit card lets you spend up to a certain limit on credit. Each month, you'll be billed for what you've spent. It is critical to try and pay off the bill in full each month. However, you are obliged to pay at least the minimal amount.

There is a direct correlation between credit card use and the five most influential aspects of a credit score. Obtaining a credit card and making timely and responsible use of it is an excellent approach to start building or repairing your credit, which, as stated above, influences your eligibility for a loan.

These are the five points that affect a credit score:

1. Payment history (35%)
2. Amounts owed (30%)
3. Length of credit history (15%)
4. New credit (10%)
5. Credit mix (10%) (mortgage, store accounts, loans, and so on)

Understanding essential phrases and concepts allow you to make more informed judgments as you navigate the world of credit cards. The essentials are as follows:

An Annual Fee is a payment set by certain credit cards in exchange for the privileges and rewards they offer; but not all credit cards charge these.

APR: APR is the cost you pay each month to borrow fees from the bank if you do not pay your credit card balance back in full. It is a variable percentage calculated at a monthly rate, however is represented as an annual rate as a way of standardising comparison figures across credit card companies.

Credit Limit: The credit limit is the total amount of money you can borrow on your credit card. The credit card company determines it based on creditworthiness, income and credit history.

Credit Scores: Most credit cards require a 700 or higher credit score. Cards with several offerings, including vacation and cash-back rewards, often require ratings of 750 or above. However, you can still get a credit card with a worse credit score from specific lenders.

Credit Score Requirements: Some credit cards are aimed at people who have little or no credit history. To maximize your chances of approval, look into credit cards that are valid for your present credit situation.

Credit Utilization Ratio: This compares the amount of credit you are now utilizing to the total amount of credit available. It is also known as the credit utilization rate or debt-to-credit ratio.

Extra Benefits: There are credit card options to facilitate a range of lifestyles and interests, whether it's a cash-back card, a travel card, a points card or a secured card.

The opportunity to earn rewards is one of the most significant features that any credit card can provide. Credit card rewards can help you save money on Internet purchases, travel expenses, gas station purchases and more. Credit card incentives usually are one of three types: cash back, points or frequent flyer miles.

Getting the most out of a credit card requires selecting the best card for you and using it correctly.

Pre-approval for a credit card may allow applicants to note their eligible cards without affecting their credit scores.

. . .

Introductory Offers: Some credit cards give introductory offers, such as a 0% APR on debt transfers or purchases for a certain period.

Penalty Fees: Penalty fees are penalties for late payments, exceeding your credit limit or violating the rules of your credit card.

The Grace Period is the time that elapses between the end of a billing cycle and the payment due date. You can fully pay off your credit card balance during this period and avoid paying interest.

Managing your Credit Card: Success Strategies

While credit cards can be helpful, responsible debt management is crucial. These methods will assist you in staying on top of your finances:

Keep Track of Your Spending: Begin by thoroughly understanding your spending profile. Study your credit card statements carefully and categorize your spending. This will assist you in identifying areas where you may cut back and make required budget modifications.

Make a Budget: A budget is essential for managing your credit card balance. Set aside a certain amount each month to pay off your credit card obligations.

Pay More Than the Required Minimum: Always try to pay more than the minimum payment on your credit card bill. Paying more than the minimum will accelerate your payback process and avoid accruing debt with interest. You will spend much more on interest over time if you merely pay the minimum, and it will take much longer to become debt-free, as the interest accumulates.

Consolidate Your Debt: If you have many credit cards with outstanding balances, debt consolidation may be an option. Consider integrating your debts by moving your balances to a single credit card with a lower interest rate or looking into debt consolidation loans. This streamlines your payments and could result in interest savings. However, you should aim to avoid needing to take this step by always paying your balance in full.

Seek Professional Assistance if Necessary: If your credit card debt becomes overpowering and progress seems impossible, consider seeking help from a credit counseling organization or a financial counselor.

Avoid Adding to your Debt: It's critical to avoid accruing extra debt while working to pay off your outstanding credit card debt.

Balance Transfers: If you have high-interest credit card debt, you can save money by moving the balance to a card with a reduced interest rate.

Adhere to the Following:

- Pay off your account balance.
- Pay bills on time.
- Check for court orders.
- Check for errors.
- Don't apply for more than one loan at a time.
- Avoid spending up to your credit limit.

You can redeem yourself after making mistakes – which happens to newbies and seasoned cardholders, but it's best not to make them in the first place.

Keep this in mind – if you're in trouble with your credit card, speak to the issuers about it and work out a repayment plan.

Pay attention to payment requests!

You could find yourself in court.

And cardless!

REWARDS & PERKS, FRAUD PROTECTION

To expand on what was mentioned earlier, you can earn points as a "frequent flyer" and then "cash in" those points to take a flight at a later stage. Many businesspeople earn a huge number of points as they often travel for their companies. This can see them being upgraded to business or first class.

You're also offered protection if the airline ceases to operate. This case, in point, happened to me personally. I had booked to travel from Johannesburg to London on a local airline. The airline went under and I couldn't get a refund as I hadn't paid with a credit card. Very annoying.

But cash back on purchases, rewards points, and frequent flyer miles are just a few of the advantages and benefits generally offered by credit cards. Most importantly, when compared to debit cards and cash, the fraud protection offered by credit cards is a clear advantage.

UNDERSTANDING DEBT

What Is Debt?

A debt is something owed by one party to another, usually money. Many individuals and businesses utilize debt (as loans) to finance major expenditures that they could not otherwise afford. It is generally repaid with interest.

How Does Debt Work?

Loans, such as mortgages, auto loans, personal loans and credit cards, are the most common types of debt. Most loans have an earmarked sum that the borrower must repay in full by a specific date, which could be months or years in the future. The loan terms will also specify the amount of interest that the borrower must pay, expressed as a percentage of the loan amount. Debt can take many forms, each with its own uses and requirements. Most types of debt are one or more of the following:

Secured Debt

Collateralized debt is a way of describing secured debt. That presumes the borrower has pledged something valuable as collateral for the debt. For a car loan, say, the vehicle is frequently used as collateral. If the borrower fails to return the money borrowed to purchase the car, the lender has the right to seize and sell it. Also, when someone gets a mortgage to buy a property, the home itself is generally used as collateral. If the borrower fails to make payments, the lender may foreclose and seize possession of the property.

Revolving Credit

Revolving debt provides the borrower with a line of credit from which they can borrow as required. Borrowers can lend up to a particular amount, pay off the obligation, and then borrow up to that amount again. Credit card debt is the most widespread instance of revolving debt.

The line of credit stays available for as long as the borrower fulfils their commitments, often by making monthly payments of at least a specific minimum amount. With a good repayment history, the revolving debt available to the borrower may increase over time.

Mortgages

A mortgage is a secured debt used to buy real estate, such as a house or apartment. Mortgages are typically repaid over long periods, such as 15 or 30 years.

Mortgages are frequently the highest debt that individuals will ever incur, aside from college loans, and they come in various forms. The two main kinds are fixed-rate mortgages and adjustable-rate mortgages, or ARMs. In the case of ARMs, the interest rate might evolve regularly, usually based on the performance of a specific index.

The *index* is a benchmark interest rate reflecting general market conditions.

Corporate Debt

Companies that need to borrow money have a range of possibilities that ordinary consumers do not. In addition to bank or other lender loans, they are frequently allowed to issue bonds and commercial paper.

Bonds are a type of debt instrument that allows a business to borrow money from investors in exchange for acknowledgement to repay the money with interest. Bonds, which generally possess a set interest rate, can be purchased by people and investment firms. If a corporation needs to raise $1 million to cover the purchase of new equipment, say, it could issue 1,000 bonds, costing $1,000 each.

Bonds often become due in the future, known as the maturity date, at which point the investor receives the bond's total value. In addition, the investor will have received regular interest payments over the years.

How to Pay Off Debt

Experts generally advise paying off your highest-interest loans first and working your way down.

For example, if you receive a promotion and therefore an increase in your salary, a high interest loan such as a mortgage can be paid off faster by increasing the amount of *capital* you pay per month, subsequently reducing the amount of interest you owe.

UNDERSTANDING INSURANCE

Insurance coverage helps consumers to rebound financially from unexpected events such as car accidents or the loss of a family's income-producing adult. The insured person pays a premium to the insurance company to benefit him or herself of this coverage. Insurance coverage and prices are frequently affected by several things, such as risk.

Managing Risk

An insurance firm manages risk by charging premiums. When there is a greater likelihood that an insurance company will have to pay money toward a claim, the risk can be addressed by charging a higher premium.

The Main Types of Insurance Protection are:

Auto Insurance Protection

In the event of a vehicle accident, auto insurance can protect you. Drivers in all 50 states, except New Hampshire, must have minimum liability insurance coverage.

Life Insurance Protection

Life insurance offers financial stability for your loved ones if you die. You can name a primary beneficiary and contingent beneficiary to receive a death benefit if you pass away. These are the people set to receive your life insurance.

Insurance for Homeowners

Homeowner's insurance protects you from financial losses caused by incidents in your house. A standard homeowner's insurance policy covers both the home and its contents in events such as fire and theft.

TAX PLANNING AND STRATEGIES

Taxes are mandatory sums laid on individuals or corporations by a government entity—whether local, regional or national. Tax incomes finance government activities, including public works and services such as roads and schools or Social Security and Medicare programs. There are various taxes to consider, including payroll, federal and state income and sales taxes. Check out the most common below:

Income Tax is a proportion of earned income paid to the state or federal government. (For example, $2 of your $12 an hour salary goes to the government.)

Payroll Tax is a sum deducted from an employee's wages and paid to the government on the employee's behalf to fund Medicare and Social Security programs. The difference between payroll and income tax is that employers do not pay income tax.

Business Tax is a government-levied (imposed) percentage of business profits used to pay federal programs.

Taxes Levied on certain commodities and services; this varies by jurisdiction.

Property Taxes are levied based on the value of land and property assets.

Tariffs are taxes levied on imported goods to strengthen domestic firms.

Estate Tax Is a tax levied on the fair market value (FMV) of property in a person's estate at the time of death. The total estate must exceed state and federal government standards.

Tax Planning Strategies and How They Work

Tax planning tactics assist taxpayers in avoiding penalties, minimizing their tax deductions, organizing their fiscal obligations (financial demands) and planning for the future, in addition to saving money. Failing to plan for taxes pulls money away from other priorities by increasing tax payments unnecessarily.

College Students

College students are particularly vulnerable to unjustified taxation because their parents no longer identify them as dependents on their tax returns and they incur student loan debt. Here are some ways tax preparation helps college students, other individuals and businesses, as well as examining the repercussions of inadequate tax planning.

Individual Tax Planning Strategies

The proverb "Watch the pennies and the dollars will take care of themselves" applies doubly to individual tax preparation tactics. College students, recent graduates and others trying to make a living can lower their tax liabilities by utilizing tax-saving alternatives offered to people of all income levels.

Understand Your Dependency Situation

The IRS (Internal Revenue Service) defines a dependent as a qualifying child or qualifying relative:

This person is a son, daughter, stepchild, foster child, brother, sister, half-brother or half-sister who is younger than the tax filer and is under 19 years old after the tax year or under the age of 24 if a student.

To qualify as a *dependent child*, the individual must have lived with the filer for more than half of the year, received more than half of the filer's support and be unable to file a joint return except to claim a refund of tax withheld or anticipated tax paid.

A *dependent relative* must be related to the filer in one of numerous ways, must live with the filer for the whole year, and have a gross income of less than $4,200 for the year.

The filer must offer more than half of the total annual assistance for the dependent relative.

For a qualifying child or qualifying relative to be claimable as a dependent, three requirements must be met:

1. The person claiming to be dependant on a tax payer cannot claim to have someone else be dependant on them.

2. A married person cannot be claimed as a dependent if they file a joint return unless they claim a refund of income tax withheld or estimated tax payment.

3. Only US citizens, US nationals or Canadian or Mexican residents can be claimed as dependents, except for adopted children.

Understand the Tax Requirements in your Home State and your School State

Even if they attend out-of-state schools, most college students return to their home states where their families live. For federal tax reasons, Intuit outlines how to determine your home state:

- The address on your driver's license.
- The state in which your vehicle is registered, as well as the state in which you are registered to vote.
- The state in which you possess property.

Out-of-state students, on the other hand, may be required to file nonresident state tax returns and pay income taxes to the states where they attend school. Students may also need to submit state tax returns in their home states, but they will receive credit for any income taxes paid to another state.

The Costs of Failure to Plan for Taxes

Individuals and organizations risk more than just a higher-than-necessary tax payment by failing to implement a tax planning strategy. If they do not pay their taxes on time, the IRS charges penalties and interest on the unpaid sum until the balance is paid in full. The IRS imposes penalties for a variety of reasons, including:

- Inability to file.
- Failure to make timely payments.
- Failure to pay the correct estimated tax.
- Check dishonored.

The IRS grants certain penalty relief to small firms and self-employed people in cases where an effort was made to comply with tax obligations, but the tax obligation was not adhered to due to circumstances beyond the taxpayer's control.

KEY TAKEAWAYS

- **The Importance of Saving and Emergency Funds – an absolute necessity.**
- **Banking Basics – know how the bank operates concerning your needs.**
- **The World of Credit Cards – they're a must, but use them wisely.**
- **The Art of Managing Debt – how to avoid Trouble with a capital "T."**
- **Understanding Insurance – know how to protect your finances**
- **Tax Planning and Strategies – it's all seemingly very complex at first, but getting used to them comes quickly**.

COMING UP

How to immerse yourself in the exciting world of investments; the road to wealth seems daunting, but not when we break it down…

DON'S SPENDING SPREE HALTED BY FRAUD

Don was a diligent person who, from nothing, had made a success of his life. To establish himself financially, he applied for his first credit card. Don's new credit card allowed him to do what he wanted, when he wanted. He used it for everything, from groceries to clothes to his dream vacation.

Despite his enthusiasm, he couldn't help but consider the risks of making a large purchase with a credit card.
Then, one day, he received a call from the bank's fraud prevention team, letting him know that they had uncovered fraudulent activity on his credit card. Don's heart pounded as he envisioned his identity being stolen and his savings being depleted.
Fortunately, his credit card has comprehensive protection against fraud. In response to the suspicious activity on Don's account, the bank moved quickly to protect his funds and launch an investigation. The bank reassured him that he would not be responsible for any bogus bills.

Don understood then how important it was to have a credit card with excellent fraud protection. It wasn't only about having the ability to make purchases quickly and easily; it was also about knowing that someone had his back if anything went wrong.
After that, he began spreading the word about the necessity of choosing a credit card with robust fraud protection measures and encouraging others to do the same. He told his tale everywhere so that people could learn from his experience and make better financial decisions.

When it is time for you to get a credit card, remember that you, too, can choose to be protected like Don, by obtaining a credit card with robust fraud protection. It pays to make prudent decisions and take precautions against the unexpected… literally!

3

INVESTING 101: THE ROAD TO WEALTH

"The speed of your success is limited only by your dedication and what you're willing to sacrifice."

— NATHAN W. MORRIS

INTRODUCTION TO INVESTING: STOCKS, BONDS, MUTUAL FUNDS

What is Investing?

Purchasing assets that appreciate (now in value) over time and offer returns in the shape of income checks or capital gains is the practice of investing. In a broader sense, investment can also mean devoting time or resources to upscaling your own or others' lives. But in the world of finance, investing refers to the act of buying stocks, real estate and other things of value to accrue money or capital gains.

Understanding Investing

The fundamental principle of investing is anticipating price appreciation (capital growth) of an asset, thus gaining a favorable return you can 'cash-out' as income. There are a broad range of assets in which one can invest and generate a return.

In investment, risk and return are inversely correlated; low risk typically translates into low predicted returns, whereas larger profits are usually associated with increased risk. Basic investments like Certificates of Deposit (CDs) are at the low end of the risk spectrum; bonds or fixed-income instruments are higher risk, whilst stocks or equities are qualified as riskier still. IPO's (Initial Public Offerings) are considered to be among the riskiest assets; these are the first shares offered when a company launches.

Aside from investing in assets like real estate or land, one can also do so in delicate things like fine art and antiques.

Within the same asset class, risk and return expectations can differ. A micro-cap (a small company that has a market capitalization between $50 million and $300 million and is considered riskier than a large-cap stock) that trades on a tiny exchange will have a substantially different risk-return profile than a blue chip company (a nationally or internationally recognized, well-established, and financially sound company that is publicly traded, like Coca Cola or Amazon) on the New York Stock Exchange.

Depending on the type of asset, different returns are produced. For instance, many equities pay dividends quarterly (every three months), whereas bonds often pay interest twice a year.

Price appreciation is a significant part of the return in addition to regular income like dividends or interest. Thus, the total return on investment is the sum of income and capital growth. According to Standard & Poor's estimates, dividends have made up about a third of the total equity return for the S&P 500 since 1926, while capital gains have made up the other two thirds.

Although there are multiple kinds of investments, the following are the most typical ones:

Stocks

A stock purchase makes the buyer a fractional owner of a company. Shareholders own a company's stock and can benefit from its expansion and success by increasing the value of their investment when the stock price goes up, and earning regular dividend payments from the company's earnings.

Bonds

Bonds are debt obligations from organizations like governments, municipalities and businesses. A bond means that you own a portion of a company's debt and are qualified to receive periodic interest payments and the face value of the bond once it matures with the promise of interest payments in return. Basically, you are lending money to a government or corporation that pay your money back plus interest.

Funds

Investment managers manage funds, which are pooled instruments that let investors buy stocks, bonds, preferred shares, commodities and the like. (It allows people to purchase multiple stocks/shares in a group of companies.) Mutual funds and exchange-traded funds, or ETFs, are two of the most popular categories of funds. ETFs trade on stock exchanges and, like stocks, regularly pause and are valued during the trading day, unlike mutual funds, which do not trade on an exchange and are evaluated at the close of the trading day. Fund managers can actively manage Mutual Funds and ETFs, or track benchmarks, like the S&P 500 or the Dow Jones Industrial Average.

The Dow Jones Industrial Average, Dow Jones, or simply the Dow, is a stock market index of 30 prominent companies listed on stock exchanges in the United States. The DJIA is one of the oldest and most commonly followed equity indexes.

Securities Trusts

Another category of pooled investment is trusts. One of the most well-known types of securities in this group is real estate investment trusts (REITs). REITs perform in residential or commercial real estate. From the rental revenue these properties generate, they pay out to their investors regularly. Due to their stock exchange trading, REITs benefit their investors from immediate *liquidity* (the ease with which an asset, or security, can be converted into ready cash without affecting its market price).

Alternative Investments

Hedge funds and private equity fall under the umbrella term of 'alternative investments'. Hedge funds are so allocated because they can utilize long and short-term stock positions and other investments to diversify their investing bets. Without becoming public, private equity enables businesses to raise finance. Typically, wealthy individuals who met particular income and net worth standards and were referred to as "accredited investors" were the only ones with access to hedge funds and private equity. Alternative investments have, however, recently been made available to retail (non-professional) investors in fund formats.

Alternative Derivatives and Options

Financial instruments, known as derivatives, produce their value from another instrument, like a stock or index. Popular derivatives, like options contracts, provide the buyer with the option, but not the duty, to purchase or sell a security at a specified price within a predetermined time window. Leverage, which is further money borrowed to purchase a stock, is frequently used in derivatives, making them a high-risk, high-reward investment.

Commodities

Along with financial instruments and currencies, commodities also include items like metals, oil, grains and animal goods. Commodity futures, which are contracts to purchase or sell a specific amount of a commodity at a given price on a particular future date, or ETFs, are the two ways they can be traded. Commodities can be traded for speculative (an investment or investment strategy that involves a relatively high degree of risk and uncertainty) or risk-hedging objectives. Risk-hedging is a strategy employed by individuals, businesses or investors to reduce the potential negative impact of adverse price movements or events in financial markets.

How to Invest

Self-Directed Investing

The answer to the question "how do I invest" depends on whether you are a Do-It-Yourself investor or would rather have a professional manage your money. Many investors who prefer to handle their funds themselves have accounts on online brokerages, due to the low commissions and simplicity of trading on these platforms.

DIY investing, or self-directed investment, calls for knowledge, expertise, time commitment and emotional restraint. It's often best to let a professional manage your money if you don't fit these descriptions.

Professionally Managed Investing

Wealth managers typically manage investments for investors who want professional money management. AUM, or Assets Under Management, refers to the total market value of all the financial assets (such as stocks, bonds, cash and other investments) that a financial institution, investment firm or an individual manages on behalf of their clients. Even though hiring an experienced money manager costs more than managing money alone, some investors are willing to pay for the fluidity and responsibility of having an expert handle the research, investment decisions and trading.

Where Do I Begin Investing?

As mentioned above, you have two options for investing: you can do it yourself and choose investments based on your investing style, or you can work with a professional, like a broker or advisor. It's crucial to ascertain your preferences and risk tolerance before investing. Stocks and options may not be the ideal choice if you are risk-averse. Devise a plan detailing how much, how frequently and what to invest in based on your objectives and preferences. Ensure the target investment aligns with your strategy and can deliver the required results before committing your resources. Remember that you don't need a lot of money to start and you can adapt your needs as you go along.

What Kinds of Investments Are There?

There are numerous investment options available. Equities, bonds, property, and ETFs/mutual funds are the most popular. Certificates of deposit, annuities, cryptocurrencies, commodities, collectables and precious metals are more investment options to consider. A financial adviser can help you plan a good investment portfolio.

BUILDING A DIVERSIFIED INVESTMENT PORTFOLIO

Investors may discover that one or two securities constitute a sizeable chunk of their whole portfolio, as stocks and other investments fluctuate in value over time. Periodically reviewing your portfolio can help ensure that your fortunes are not dependent on just one or two investments by increasing diversification.

What is Diversification?

Diversification is a way to manage risk in your portfolio by investing in various asset classes.

Diversification is a crucial part of any investment plan. It is ultimately an acknowledgement that the future is uncertain and no one knows exactly what will happen. If you knew the future, you would not need to diversify your investments, however by doing so, you'll be better prepared for the inevitable peaks and valleys of investing.

Three Ideas to Help you Create a Varied Portfolio:

Creating a balanced portfolio might seem daunting with so many investment options. Here are three suggestions that make diversification simple for novices:

1. Purchase an index fund or at least 25 equities from various industries.

Purchasing an index fund is a smart way to achieve diversification for folks who don't have the time to investigate stocks. For instance, an S&P 500 index fund will try to replicate the performance of the S&P 500. The advantage of index funds is that they immediately diversify investments and remove much of the uncertainty involved in investing. For instance, when you purchase an S&P 500 index fund share, you gain exposure to 500 of the biggest publicly traded U.S. firms.

Another significant benefit of index funds is their extremely low-cost ratios. This is so that you can invest in index funds without paying a fund manager to conduct research and select investments for you.

Buying numerous stocks is one of the quickest ways to create a diversified portfolio. The golden rule is to own at least 25 separate businesses that come from a *variety* of industries. Though it may be alluring to buy stock in a dozen well-known IT behemoths and call a halt to your investing, this is not diversification. All those companies' shares may drop simultaneously if tech spending suffers due to new government rules or a slowdown in the economy.

2. Make a little investment in fixed income.

Putting money into fixed-income assets like bonds can be another method towards portfolio diversification. Fixed income refers to a group of assets and securities that give investors a set amount of cash flows, usually in the form of regular interest or dividends.

The most popular types of fixed-income products are government and company bonds.

They are called "fixed-income" because the interest rate paid to buyers is always the same.

While adding some bonds lowers a portfolio's average yearly rate of return, it also tends to limit the number of years with losses and therefore, limit the loss of the worst year.

There are simple ways to gain some fixed-income exposure, even if choosing bonds might be much more complicated than selecting equities. One of these is to purchase an exchange-traded fund (ETF) that focuses on bonds.

3. Take into account putting some money into real estate.

Real estate should be added to the mix for investors who want to diversify their holdings further. In the past, real estate has boosted a portfolio's overall return while lowering its volatility (tendency to change).

Investing in real estate investment trusts (REITs), which own real estate with income potential, is a simple way of doing this. The industry has a successful history. As determined by the 'FTSE Nareit, All Equity REIT Index', REITs outperformed the S&P 500 in 15 of the 25 years that ended in 2019 and had an average annual total return of 10.9%.

According to several studies, an ideal portfolio will allocate 5% to 15% of its assets to REITs. For instance, a portfolio comprising 80% equities, 20% bonds and 10% REITs has historically outperformed a portfolio comprising 60% stocks and 40% bonds, with only slightly greater volatility. It has also matched the returns of portfolios consisting of 55% stocks, 35% bonds and 10% REITs.

It's estimated that 90% of millionaires invest in real estate in some form, so it should certainly be in your long term plans if this level of income is your goal.

Compound Interest

> *"Compound interest is the eighth wonder of the world. He who understands it, earns it; he who doesn't, pays it."*

> — ALBERT EINSTEIN

Money gained on your principal investment, as well as the gains that the investment makes over time, is known as compound interest. This means if you receive returns on your investment, those gains may also generate further profits if reinvested. Because the returns component of your portfolio continually produces more money, compound interest leads to exponential payoffs.

How to Calculate Compound Interest

Let's say you had $1000 today and put it in a portfolio with a 5% annual return on average. That $1000 would bring in $50 in a year (1000 x 0.05). If you then *reinvest* that $50, you would make $52,50 in the second year (1050 x 0.05), $55,13 (1102.50 x 0.05) in the third year, and so on.

Compound interest only favours your investments when the returns are reinvested. Using the figures from above, you would only make $50 annually if you had taken all the profits from your interest.

Compound interest provides enormous gains over the long term, as evidenced by the following diagrams. Say you start with $1000 dollars; in 20 years you will have $3000 based on 10% interest *not* compounded, meaning you take any interest payments away from the investment pool. Compound interest, in contrast, would leave you with over $7000 dollars. Over 40 years the same principle changes that final sum from $5000 to a whopping $53,000.

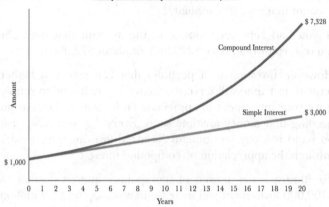

Compound vs Simple Interest - 20 years

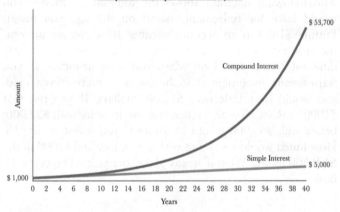

Compound vs Simple Interest - 40 years

Start Investing Early to Benefit from Compound Interest

You could assume that a minor difference in returns wouldn't impact a person's wealth much. But know this: 1% more in returns can significantly impact how much money you will have in the long run.

In 40 years, $100,000 in an account earning 1% annually would only increase to roughly $148,886. What would

59

happen if someone transferred that money to a savings account that paid 2% annually?

If you had kept your money in the account that paid 2% interest, you would have $220,803, or about $72,000 more.

However, investing in a portfolio that can give you higher returns over time will serve you better if you intend to simply leave your investment to appreciate on its own and can avoid needing that money anytime soon. Every day you have cash on hand is a day you potentially avoid growing your wealth through the appreciation of compound interest.

To illustrate the power of compound interest further, a $100,000 investment will increase to a whopping $1.9 million in 40 years with an average annual return of 7.64%.

The following diagram shows the amount of money you would have for retirement, based on the age you invest. Putting $1000 in an account earning 10% average interest, the historical average of the S&P 500, shows significantly different results based on when you start investing. If you started your investment at 35, by the time you're 60 years old, you would have little over $12,000 dollars. If you put that $1000 to work 10 years earlier, you would retire with $32,000; better still, $63,000 would be yours if you invest at age 18. How much would you retire with if you invested $1000 in the S&P 500 today? What if it was $1000 per year? The sky is the limit.

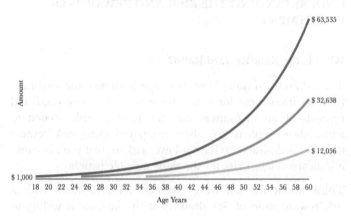

Compound Interest Saving 18 vs. 25 vs. 35

Invest for as Long as you Can

It can be tempting to sell investments when the market declines or even to hold onto funds while trying to time out the market (selling for the most profit possible).

However, the power of compounding only manifests itself when you have the resolve to ride out market fluctuations without touching your investments. Remembering that investing involves knowing you're in it for the long run is critical. The key to successful long-term investing is a view without a visible horizon.

Although the value of your portfolio will fluctuate in the short term, it is ultimately preferable to maintain an investment portfolio that outperforms inflation.

Furthermore, nobody is ever going to time the market perfectly. The stock market has a history of rising over a longer period. It is preferable to ride it out for as long as you can.

UNDERSTANDING THE RISK AND REWARDS OF INVESTMENT

What is the Risk/Reward Ratio?

The risk/reward ratio shows how much an investor might get from an investment for every dollar they risk. The predicted rewards of an investment and the level of risk needed to attain those returns are often compared using risk/reward ratios. It is desirable to have a lower risk/return ratio because it indicates a lesser risk for the same possible benefit.

Think about the following instance: an investment with a risk/reward ratio of 1:7 shows that the investor is willing to take a $1 risk in exchange for the chance to make a $7 profit. In the same way, an investor should anticipate investing $1 with the potential to gain $3 in return if the risk/reward ratio is 1:3.

The ratio is calculated by dividing the amount a trader stands to lose if the price of an asset moves in an unexpected direction (the risk) by the amount of profit the trader expects to have made when the position is closed (the reward). Traders frequently use this approach to plan which trades to take.

Risk/return ratio = Potential loss/Potential gain

Investors can determine whether a proposed investment is worthwhile by using risk/return ratios; ultimately making better investment decisions and handling risk skillfully and safely.

How the Risk/Reward Ratio works

Market strategists generally agree that the best risk/reward ratio for their investments is around 1:3, or three units of projected return for every additional unit of risk. Stop-loss orders and derivatives like 'put options' (an option to sell assets at an agreed price on or before a particular date) allow investors to manage risk and profit.

A put option gives you the right, but not the commitment, to sell a stock at a certain price (known as the strike price) by a specific time – at the option's expiration. For this right, the put buyer pays the seller a sum of money called a premium.

The risk/reward ratio is frequently used as a gauge while trading individual equities. Many investors will have a pre-specified risk/reward ratio for their assets in the same way different trading systems will; both typically calculated by a trial-and-error approach.

Be aware that risk/return ratios can be calculated subjectively (based on an investor's risk tolerance) and objectively (using an investment's risk/return profile). In the latter scenario, the possible loss is frequently employed as the numerator and the predicted return as the denominator. It is possible to calculate expected returns in many different ways, such as by embedding past returns into the future, calculating the weighted probabilities of potential outcomes, or applying a model like the Capital Asset Pricing Model (CAPM).

Examination of a company's financial statements, technical analysis of previous price data, value-at-risk (VaR) models and other techniques can all be used by investors to determine the possible loss. These techniques can assist investors in identifying variables that may affect an investment's value and in calculating the potential risk.

Can the Risk/Return Ratio of an Investment Change Over Time?

Yes, since the investment's price moves and its potential risk changes, the risk/return ratio can alter with time. For instance, if the price of a stock increases, the *potential* return may be lower than when it was first bought. Yet, the potential risk may also have increased.

To ensure that your investments align with your objectives and risk tolerance, it's crucial to routinely assess your holdings' risk/return ratio and modify your portfolio as necessary.

There are several different funds with various risk profiles from which to pick. Some hold bonds, some hold gold and other precious metals, some hold shares in foreign firms, some hold large-company stocks, some blend large- and small-company equities and some own just about any other asset kind you can think of. Although mutual funds don't eliminate risk, you can utilize them to protect yourself from the risk associated with other investments.

Typical Investment Risks:

Money Loss

The most typical risk is that your investment will be a financial loss. You can make investments that promise no losses, but in exchange, you'll give up most of your chance to get a respectable return.

For instance, the United States government backs U.S. Treasury bonds and bills, making them one of the safest securities in the entire world. Bank certificates of deposit (CDs) held at a bank with federal deposit insurance are, likewise, safe. However, the cost of this safety comes at a very poor rate of return on your investment.

Your investment may yield very little growth when you include the effects of inflation and the taxes you pay on your gains.

Missing Your Financial Objectives

The amount of money and time invested, rate of return or growth, fees, taxes and inflation are factors that affect whether you meet your investing goals. You'll probably get a smaller investment return if you can only afford to take a few risks, as often you need to spend more money and time to make up for it. However, this isn't necessarily a bad thing, as it's great to exercise caution when you're first starting out.

Similarly, if you are five years away from retirement, you don't want to take any chances with your nest egg because you will likely have less time left and resources to recoup from a significant loss.

While failing to reach your financial objectives is technically a risk, it is of course subjective to your priorities. It's always worth reviewing your objectives to adjust them if you suddenly face significant changes to your personal or career circumstances.

REAL ESTATE INVESTING

> *"Ninety percent of all millionaires become so through owning real estate. More money has been made in real estate than in all industrial investments combined. The wise young man or wage earner of today invests his money in real estate."*

> — ANDREW CARNEGIE

Real Estate for Beginners

If done correctly, real estate investing may produce generational wealth (assets passed down from one generation to the next) and outperform the stock market by a wide margin. There are three primary ways to profit from real estate ownership: rental income, capital gains and dividends from holding REIT shares.

There are numerous ways to invest in real estate. A person can first buy a home with capital, either alone or by pooling funds with others.

A real estate investment trust is another option; these are publicly traded businesses that own and manage properties. As a result, shares can be purchased and sold just like any other stock.

One can also put money into an online real estate market-place like Crowdstreet or Fundraise. Only accredited investors are permitted on some of these platforms, however, they link investors wishing to participate in real estate projects with developers and operators.

Alternatively, crowdfunding is accessible to anyone wishing to start. Crowdfunding is the practise of raising money with a group of others, with each personal contributing a small amount; this is typically done online. Say you choose to put $10,000 into a $100,000 crowdfunded property. Consequently, you formally own 10% of the property. If it produces a net rental yield of 6% over a year, that amounts to $6,000, of which you receive 10%, or $600.

Additionally, any auxiliary revenue a person can generate from their home is another clever way to profit. For instance, one might install a vending machine or a small laundry facility at their apartment building. Cleverer still you could earn money by charging a management fee for looking after these assets.

Lets explore the best ways to invest in real estate:

1. Consider purchasing a rental property

When Tiffany Alexy purchased her first rental property at 21, she had no intention of becoming a real estate investor. She was a senior in college in Raleigh, North Carolina, and had plans to attend Graduate School there. She reasoned that purchasing would be preferable to renting.

"I searched Craigslist and discovered a four-bedroom, four-bath condo that was furnished in a manner reminiscent of student accommodation. I purchased it, lived in one bedroom and rented out the other three", says Alexy.

For a graduate student, the arrangement was far from pocket change, generating an additional $1000 a month: certainly enough for Alexy to get the real estate itch.

Alexy entered the market utilizing a technique known as "house hacking," coined by the online portal for real estate investors, BiggerPockets. By renting out rooms, as Alexy did, or apartments in a multi-unit complex, you are occupying your investment property. According to David Meyer, the site's Vice President of statistics and analytics, investors can employ house hacking to purchase a building with up to four apartments while still being eligible for a residential loan.

Of course, you could also purchase a whole investment property and rent it out without living there yourself, ideally where the total costs are less than the rent you can charge. You'll also need to pay a property manager to avoid being the one who calls for help for a leak or worse, has to show up with a toolbelt!

"If you manage it yourself, you'll learn a lot about the industry, and if you buy future properties, you'll go into it with more experience," Meyer advises.

2. Capital gains

There are two ways to receive capital gains through an investment property.

Property prices tend to appreciate over time, with the occasional market fluctuation, therefore simply purchasing a house or apartment will produce capital gains. This can be 'left' in the house as equity, or liquidated into available cash by selling; the latter of which people do when renovating or *house flipping*.

This is HGTV in real life: you buy a cheap house that needs some work, renovate it as cost effectively as you can and then sell it for a profit. This tactic is a little more complicated than it appears on TV, given the current increase in the cost of building materials and mortgage interest rates. While it unfortunately has become more expensive than it used to be, it is still lucrative as the goal of many home flippers is to pay cash for the properties.

Because the calculations of how much repairs would cost need to be so exact, which is a complex thing to accomplish, there is a greater degree of risk, according to Meyer. He advises to "find a partner with experience who is good at budgeting or project management, while you "have resources to contribute, like money and time".

The other risk of flipping is that you could lose money if you hold the home for an extended period since you would have to pay the mortgage without receiving any revenue. You can reduce that risk by residing in the house while it is being renovated. This works as long as most of the upgrades are cosmetic and you don't mind a little dust.

3. Purchasing REITs

Investing in REITs (Real Estate Investment Trusts) is an ideal way for beginners to start real estate investing. Compared to the equity needed to buy an entire home, someone can purchase shares for a lot less. Additionally, they can review quarterly reports to understand the stock's performance better and sharpen their real estate investment skills. REITs are businesses that own commercial real estate, such as office buildings, retail spaces, apartments and hotels. They are frequently compared to mutual funds. Due to their tendency to pay substantial dividends, REITs are a popular choice for retirement investments. Investors can automatically reinvest those dividends to increase the value of their investment if they do not want or desire regular income.

Are REITs a wise financial choice? While they might be, they can also be varied and complex. Some are not publicly traded, while others are moved on an exchange like stocks. Given that non-traded REITs are challenging to sell and may be difficult to evaluate, the type of REIT you choose to invest in can significantly impact the level of risk you assume.

In general, it is advised that novice investors should stick to publicly traded REITs, which you buy through brokerage companies, however for that, you will require a brokerage account. Don't fear though, opening one takes less than 15 minutes and many companies don't demand an initial investment (though the REIT itself probably will).

By investing in a fund with holdings in numerous REITs, you can benefit from a more diversified selection of real estate investments. You may accomplish this by purchasing shares of a mutual fund that owns REITs or investing in a real estate ETF.

Risks and Rewards

Although real estate investing can be profitable, it's necessary to be aware of the risks. The main hazards are bad sites, poor cash flows, long periods of vacancies and problematic renters. The real estate market's unpredictability, latent structural issues and lack of liquidity are additional dangers to consider.

KEY TAKEAWAYS

- **Investing refers to the act of buying stocks, real estate and other things of value to accrue money or capital gains.**
- **Increasing Diversification - don't put all your eggs in one basket and periodically review your portfolio to help ensure that your fortunes are not dependent on just one or two investments.**
- **Compound Interest - the exponential growth of investment and re-investment over time.**
- **Risk/Reward Ratios - the predicted rewards of an investment against the level of risk needed to attain those rewards.**

COMING UP

An introduction to the world of entrepreneurship; learning how to make the most of all the opportunities out there, building your business plan, and how to market and sell your products to the right audience.

LEANNE - THE TEEN STAR OF REAL ESTATE

Leanne had never known a real home. After her parents died in an car accident when she was very young, she had been passed from foster home to foster home.

Even at the young age of ten years old, she was fascinated by the grand residences in her city. At night, she would gaze up at the windows of homes, basking in their light and listening to the laughter from the rooms within.

"That must be a bedroom," she thought. She could stay here all night, pretending she was in there too.

Suddenly, a man's voice came from what she guessed was the sitting room.

"Hey!" he shouted. "What do you want?"

She took off, crying.

"I'm so pathetic," she thought. At least houses couldn't yell at her. They were safe, lovely things.

When she was 16, she decided to put her plans of selling homes into action. "Dream on, Leanne," she said to herself. "How you ever gonna do that?"

Well, upon turning 18, she went to an open house and spoke to someone who looked like he was in charge.

She went up to him and said: "Hi, my name is Leanne."

He was writing something in a folder, stopped and looked up, smiling. "Hi, Leanne. Interested in buying this place?"

She blushed a deep scarlet. "Oh, right," she said sarcastically.

"Actually, I want to know what it takes to be like you."

"Are you serious?"

She nodded.

He gave her his card. "Call me at the office, and you can come in for a chat, okay?"

She took the card. "Thank you".

Leanne called the next day.

The guy's name was Bradley and he was very nice. He told her to drop in for some coffee.

She did and she spilled her guts about being in a foster home and had always wanted a home of her own. But she realized if she couldn't buy one, she'd sell them.

Brad was amazed at the change in her; when talking about homes, she became very animated—a completely different person.

He found out she had left the last foster home "for good", she had said defiantly, and was living with a friend from school and her parents.

Brad knew there was something extraordinary about this girl.

Long story short, he and his wife Alice took her under their wing.

She studied for the Ohio Real Estate Realtors exam online and passed with flying colors.

Alice and Brad took her shopping for some smart clothes. On her first day, wearing one of her new outfits, Brad couldn't believe she had been the nervous girl he had met.

"I can't thank you enough", she said.

He offered her a job at his business. She couldn't believe it. At 18!

It turned out that she, almost instantly, became their best salesperson. She was an absolute natural and converted virtually all her specs.

At 23, she was able to buy her own tiny home. Her happiness overflowed into every room in her special hideout.

"You're all mine," she whispered. "I'll never let you go."

But she did, of course.

When she bought a bigger place!

4

STRATEGIES FOR TEENAGE ENTREPRENEURS

"My biggest motivation? Just to keep challenging myself. I see life almost like one long University education that I never had -- every day I'm learning something new."

— RICHARD BRANSON

⑤

F EEDING THE FIRE OF FULFILLMENT

The fire of finance has begun to burn within you, which, as a teen, can become a wondrous thing. Becoming an entrepreneur could be one of the most exciting choices for your future, as creating your own business could well become an empire!

But first, you must plan so well that you can recite your strategy in your sleep. Every entrepreneur began just as you are starting, with baby steps.

I know how you're feeling. You are so full of ideas and eager to change the world that you're just about to burst. Don't do that. Picking up the pieces might not be that great.

At this stage, your business is a blueprint that has begun to blossom and by first building a solid foundation, we can refine and develop it into what will become something magnificent.

THE ENTREPRENEURIAL MINDSET: IDEAS AND OPPORTUNITIES

What qualities define an excellent teen business idea?

A few requirements will make a business idea simpler for you to launch and run. You will likely have a rigorous class schedule and probably few resources for startup finances, so check out the criteria below that can offer some helpful business suggestions:

1. Based at home or conveniently located

Depending on your age, travel may be an issue. A home-based and registered company will be considerably simpler to run if you are yet to drive or still learning.

2. Convenient hours

Even though school isn't seen as "employment," depending on your extracurricular activities, it does take up to 8 to 10 hours each weekday, making it equivalent to working a full-time job. Bearing this in mind, the ideal venture will allow you to work on the weekends or throughout alternative flexible hours.

3. Minimal financial outlay

Most aspiring entrepreneurs want to invest as much money as possible in their new venture. Still, many of you will have little savings and access to outside finance (especially if you don't want the "bank of mom and dad" to be continually badgered). The secret to success is picking a business idea that needs a small financial investment. The less you need to buy before starting the business, the fewer items are required to run it.

Some Great Business Ideas for Teens

> *"Find a job you enjoy doing and you will never have to work a day in your life."*

> — MARK TWAIN

It would be best to choose something you enjoy, otherwise, your efforts will become pointless. Refrain from following something that someone else made a success of and think, okay, I can do that. Sure, you can do that, but it's not what gets you up in the morning. Choose wisely. There will be times where it is hard and it feels like no progress is being made; you'll only be able to continue if you enjoy it. If you want to use a business or an idea as a stepping stone, that's okay as long as it moves you forward to your real goal. Time is precious. Others may not have the opportunities that you have, so make the most of what you've got. It's up to you.

Here are some suggestions:

Academic Coach

You can start a simple, low-cost business by becoming an academic tutor. Everyone has a set of unique talents; whether you excel in math, science, writing or reading, you can help others who may be having trouble with the topics. An academic tutor can also assist with test preparation for the SATs, ACTs, AP exams or other standardized tests. Reach out to family friends, talk to your parents or deliver leaflets in your local town.

Car Washing

Everyone wants their car to look brand-new and glossy. Still, only some have time to get their vehicle all sparkly. Simple items are required to start a car washing business, including a bucket, soft sponge, window cleaner and elbow grease for polishing. You can do this as a fun weekend job.

Car washing was my very first business venture at 12 years old. I made a list of everything I needed to buy: a bucket, sponge, interior cleaner, etc. I printed off some flyers with a list of services and went door to door in my local town. Whilst I only did a few cars, and only paid off the startup costs, it was a great experience and gave me the entrepreneurial buzz. It helped that I had a love of cars, which is why it's crucial to do something you enjoy.

Childcare

Running a childcare or babysitting business is a tried-and-true business plan for teenagers. You can assist neighbors or friends of the family by tending to their small children on the weekends or even after school during the week. Numerous local communities provide babysitting and childcare classes if you want to stand out from the competitors. This is another business with zero start-up costs.

I also babysat for local families throughout my later teens, mostly during evenings and sometimes mornings before school. It was a great way to earn extra cash relatively easily. Sometimes, the kids even put themselves to bed and entertained themselves! The great thing about babysitting is that more work can come from recommendations in the community. Do an excellent job for one family and more work will likely come.

Dog Walking or Pet Sitting

Launching a pet-sitting or dog-walking service is the best business for kids who love spending time with animals. Both of these activities have flexible hours and your customers will supply all the necessary materials, including leashes, treats and other items.

. . .

Lawn Maintenance

The abilities required for this job are those you likely already possess if mowing the lawn is one of your chores. You can build a sizable list of clients with regular work by advertising your services in the neighbourhood. The summer is a particularly busy season for lawn care businesses and you will have plenty of free time.

I used to earn $15 for mowing my neighbors lawn in my early teens so take it from me, it works!

Cleaning the Home

Any child assisting with household duties is probably already familiar with all the abilities required to launch a house-cleaning service. Homeowners in the area will be pleased to pay a teenager to vacuum, mop and dust their house.

Housesitting Business

Many families take the opportunity to travel over the summer and during school breaks. They need someone to drop by the house while they're gone to pick up the mail, water the plants and do odd jobs. Teenagers might start a housesitting business to make additional cash while meeting a neighbourhood's needs.

Running Errands

Offering to run errands for neighbors or friends could be a simple way for teenagers who drive to launch a business and earn money. People confined to their homes or with limited mobility may find this service extremely beneficial. This business concept doesn't require any professional expertise.

. . .

Offering Handmade Goods

Teens with artistic potential talented in crafts can improve their skills and earn money by selling their products. This can be a regional business or online as a website.

- **Greeting cards** are one type of handcrafted product that teenagers can produce and market. Handwritten notes are becoming more and more popular. Teens can easily make money selling greeting cards for friends and family by creating distinctive ideas or eye-catching artwork. You can network this in your neighborhood.
- **Candles** are an easy-to-make product that are always in demand. This sellable craft is simple to learn and doesn't require a sizable initial investment, making it a good choice for teen startup business ideas.

Art Instructor

Just like the capacity to work out challenging mathematical calculations, the ability to draw, paint or create any other form of art is a skill. Teens who are talented artists looking for a business concept should consider opening an art school or class. They could share knowledge with neighboring kids who are younger or their peers.

Musician

Some artists have musical talent and spend hours honing their skills. The teenage years offer a chance for those passionate about music to gather with friends, establish a band and play at local venues. Teens should have a lot of fun with this great business idea, for example creating and selling band merchandise.

. . .

Music Instruction

Teens with a passion for music who don't wish to form a band may be interested in teaching music. There will always be a market for exceptional musicians, whether they play the piano, guitar, violin or any other instrument.

I grew up learning French horn and piano and considered teaching in the local community for a fee. Whilst it never took off, as I ended up studying away from home, there was undoubtedly a market for it and it would have played to my strengths as a musician.

Vendor at a Farmers' Market

Farmers' markets are typically excellent places to sell locally created goods and provide a simple setting for teenagers to launch their businesses. There are several opportunities for this kind of business, whether it be selling handmade goods, food or crafts. Remember that you might require a parent to make the booth reservation and manage the event.

Shopping Arbitrage

Retail arbitrage is a fun and easy business venture for teenagers. It can be a straightforward business that generates a respectable return for those who are tech-savvy online. The fundamental goal of retail arbitrage is to purchase high-quality goods at a discount and then resell them for a profit in a different market. Finding products at nearby garage sales and reselling them on eBay or Facebook Marketplace are common practices used by people who start a retail arbitrage business.

Graphic Artist

There is a chance for a tech-savvy kid who is also artistically inclined to launch a graphic design company. This can be as easy as coming up with a few great designs and printing them on T-shirts for pals, or it could entail working as a freelance marketer for local companies. Many new apps can help you on your way to becoming a top graphic designer.

Technology Teacher

While some older folks struggle to operate their computers, smartphones or tablets, the new generation have grown up with technology and are experts in this area. You could become a technology tutor and earn additional cash if you have the patience and abilities.

Blogging/Vlogging

You can start a business through blogging or vlogging with technical know-how, writing talent and a passion for a subject. Remember that this business concept will take some time to become profitable. You must first expand your audience before having the chance to work with ads and affiliate partners to generate income. But if you can optimize your blogs or vlogs, this can be a way to earn some extra cash.

Podcaster

The podcast industry is relatively new but gaining momentum rapidly throughout the US. Like a blog, you must be passionate about a subject and have a sizeable audience. You may find sponsors willing to advertise your podcasts and start making money. Note: you have to market your podcast so people know about it. Use all social media platforms to achieve your reach. There are many sites online which give straightforward ways of how to achieve your goal.

Influencers on Social Media

Most of you know that many personalities profit from promoting goods on their social media channels. Currently, this is referred to as a social media influencer. Many businesses seek out popular local figures in their markets. You might have a business on your hands if you are outgoing and willing to spend a lot of time and energy marketing yourself and a product or service.

Livestreaming Gamer

Making money while playing video games is ideal for those who enjoy gaming. Gamers who stream live do just that. Twitch is one of the most well-liked platforms for launching this kind of business.

Photographer and/or Videographer

Teens can launch a photography or videography business with a little investment in equipment or with some smartphone proficiency. A great place to start is by specializing in pet photography, events, family photographs or producing social media content for local businesses. This type of company has various specialties—an excellent start for a budding entrepreneur.

Web Designer

This young people's business idea can get you flying. Many small businesses want websites but lack the funds to engage a specialist. You can launch your own web design company by providing your skills at a reduced price. This is an excellent way to hone your abilities and earn some extra cash. Market yourself by dropping flyers off at neighboring businesses or placing a small ad in a local newspaper.

Transcription

Interview transcription for a local newspaper or company is another flexible-hours business venture. You can practice typing while also offering a service that generates income and offers an introduction into the world of journalism.

· · ·

Entering Data

You will need to know how to utilize spreadsheets and work with data for most of your upcoming careers. You might launch a data entry business once you have developed these skills. You can learn valuable new skills and have a flexible work schedule in this business.

Produce an Internet Game or App

In today's world, anyone, especially teenagers, can create an app or online game. You can start a business with a brilliant idea and the technological know-how to make it happen. Completed games and apps can subsequently be published on different app stores, with a portion of the revenue going to the developer.

Social Media Marketing Business

You can start a social media marketing business and help clients reach their target audience, creating successful campaigns and learning valuable online marketing skills for your future careers.

Making Cakes

Those of you who enjoy baking can launch your own cake-making business, letting your imagination run wild with designs while earning money. People are often looking to buy custom order cakes for events, birthday parties and cele-brations.

The Theater

So, here's something less discussed; we know that so many young adults yearn to be acting or dancing on a stage or even be a stage manager. You've participated in every school production and can't wait for the next one. You have talent and can't think of doing anything else. Many scholarships are open for students to join theater schools. This is a competitive choice, so you must have the guts and determination to enter this world. Drama and dance schools are your first stop for anything in the arts, theater, movies or television. So, get moving, and get your name up in lights!

FROM IDEA TO EXECUTION – CREATING A BUSINESS PLAN

A business plan is a written document that details your company's financial objectives and describes how you'll meet them. A solid, thorough plan will offer a roadmap for the company's upcoming three to five years, and you can share it with prospective investors, lenders or other partners. You'll find some examples at the end of this chapter.

How to Register your Company

Consult a US business lawyer licensed to practice in the state where your business is located in the US. You'll need to go through the following:

- Choose the state where your LLC (Limited Liability Company) will be incorporated.
- Locate a nearby registered agent.
- Register your LLC or S-corporation, as appropriate.
- Ask for an EIN (Employer Identification Number).
- Obtain a US mailing address if necessary.
- Open a bank account for the business.
- Open a merchant account to enable payment processing from clients.
- Get commercial insurance.
- Allocate your new company with a local phone number.
- Do some research to determine your potential tax liability.

- Make sure to keep your personal and business accounts separate.
- Pay any other needed fees as well as annual fees.
- Verify that you adhere to local, regional, state and federal regulations.
- Consult a US business attorney admitted to practice in the US state where your company is based.

Note: Your business lawyer will tell you if your business does not qualify for all the above steps. It's essential to know the facts from the very beginning.

The Importance of a Business Plan

There are several reasons to think about creating a business plan:

Planning: Besides helping you comprehend the breadth of your business and the amount of time, money and resources you'll need to get started, writing down your strategy is a beneficial exercise for forming your ideas.

Assessing Concepts: If you have many ideas in mind, creating a preliminary business plan for each will assist you in concentrating your time and efforts on the projects with the best potential of succeeding.

Research: To devise a business plan, you must conduct market and competitor research—knowledge that will guide your strategic decision-making.

Partnerships: It will be much simpler for them to decide whether your business is a good fit for theirs if you plan before approaching other businesses for collaboration. You must clearly understand your vision, your audience and your growth strategy—especially if they're further along in their growth trajectory than you are.

Competitions: Numerous business plan competitions award incentives such as mentorships, grants or investment funding. Try Googling "business plan competition + [your location]" and "business plan competition + [your industry]" to locate relevant competitions in your field. A business plan is a great place to start if you're searching for an organized strategy to arrange your thoughts and ideas and communicate them with those who can significantly impact your success.

MARKETING AND SELLING – REACHING YOUR TARGET AUDIENCE

Identify your Audience

You must first identify your target audience to reach them. You must understand your clients so you can do this correctly.

To achieve this, create a consumer persona. A generic description of your ideal customers will be a great start.

List their preferences and demographic and psychographic (individuals' psychological characteristics, interests, attitudes, values, beliefs and lifestyles.) characteristics to understand your target audience better.

Then you can market your company and its goods to people who are interested in them. As a result, there will be a greater likelihood of leads and conversions. By doing this, you can make more money with less investment.

Produce Valuable and Relevant Content

Providing your target audience with relevant and helpful material is the best method of attracting, and importantly retaining, their attention.

You will find connecting with and engaging your target audience simpler if your content marketing is more focused and relevant.

You can produce leads and conversions with the aid of content marketing. You can use it in various ways to achieve the desired outcomes. Here are a few of the most popular techniques:

. . .

Video Marketing - Videos have a very interactive and engaging quality. A high-quality video can quickly grab the audience's attention. Make sure it's short and sensational.

Blog Posts and Articles - While written material may not be as effective as movies and photos, it still helps capture your audience's attention. Just be sure the subjects you write about are interesting and helpful to your intended audience.

Social Media Content - Social media platforms are another way to reach your target audience. You can communicate with them more effectively and engage them with a combination of text, graphics and videos.

Leverage Influencers

Influencer marketing has quickly become the go-to style for digital marketers. You can use social media influencers' power to reach your target audience more effectively. In this form of marketing, you partner with influencers to market your brand to their audiences.

Influencer marketing is a very effective marketing technique that can help you attain numerous marketing goals.

If you partner with relevant influencers from your niche, you can reach potential customers who might be interested in your brand. This allows for qualified lead generation and helps you reach your target audience.

Software like GRIN can make influencer marketing easy for you. You can search for influencers and even contact them and send them sample products.

A well-managed and executed influencer marketing campaign can help your brand reach out to more people. You can extend your reach, generate leads and drive sales without breaking the bank.

. . .

Utilize Targeted Advertising

By implementing tailored advertising, you can more success-fully contact your intended audience. Whether using social networks or Google ads, each offers sophisticated targeting tools to help you find your target market. You can target the adverts based on the audience's demographics, geographic area and interests.

This will guarantee that only people likely to be interested in your brand will see your adverts. It means that reaching your target demographic, who are more likely to convert than anyone else, doesn't require you to spend a fortune on advertising.

For instance, you can design and run ads using various targeting methods on Facebook. They even provide analytics so you can improve your marketing strategies even more. Instagram and Twitter are two examples of social media sites that have their own advertising tools.

Referral Marketing

Many companies use a referral program to increase their customers and activate leads. You can leverage the strength of your existing client base to expand your reach by imple-menting a referral system, where *existing* customers recom-mend your product or service to *potential* customers. You can offer a referral code to your clients and reward them for spreading the word. You can rapidly and cheaply contact your target audience in this manner.

Naturally, you are free to experiment with your rewards. Give your new user and the referrer a discount or even a unique offer. This encourages both the new consumer and the referral to make another purchase from you.

The individuals who sign up using such a technique might be enthusiastic about your company and its goods. Businesses have benefited from using this technique to expand and build their networks.

· · ·

Use Hashtags to Connect with your Target Audience on Social Media

Social media platforms are crucial for reaching your target audience because consumers spend time on these apps. However, you must employ hashtags to target potential customers for your brand.

You can increase the audience for your social media material by using targeted, sector-specific hashtags.

A premium hotel chain, for instance, might use the hashtags #luxurytraveler or #luxurytravel. Doing this lets you connect with people interested in using your services.

Also, keep in mind that specialized hashtags are preferable to generic ones. Using general hashtags like #travelblogger or #traveler for the hotel example may be unsuccessful as it's quite broad.

BUILDING A PERSONAL BRAND AND CREATING ADDITIONAL INCOME STREAMS

For freelancers and entrepreneurs, building a personal brand has never been more critical than it is today. Anyone with access to the Internet and social media can build an audience, position themselves as an expert and start attracting clients for their business - and that's precisely what many people are doing.

The way the public perceives a person is shaped by their brand. Building your reputation, presenting a positive image to the public and promoting yourself as an individual are all important components of personal branding. Your brand is the narrative spread about you while you are absent.

It may feel uncomfortable to think of yourself as a brand. But the truth is that everyone already has a personal brand. What do people say about your work? What adjectives do they use to describe you? Are they positive or critical?

Your story is also being told online. What's being said about you in the virtual space? You can actively manage your brand or leave it to chance.

Your brand sets you apart from your rivals. Hopefully, it will leave a positive impression on your target audience and clients. With a solid personal brand that appeals to your target market, developing a successful and long-lasting company will be easier.

Building a personal brand will allow you to tell your story as you want it to be told, establish yourself as an expert and leader in your field, and connect with your customers and clients beyond your products and services alone.

Richard Branson is a good example. When compared to the Twitter accounts of his companies, Virgin Atlantic (556K), Virgin Galactic (171K) and Virgin Media (225K), he has 11.3 million followers. His bio describes himself as a "tie-loathing adventurer, philanthropist and troublemaker, who believes in turning ideas into reality." Branson leverages his brand to promote his various businesses and attract investors.

A key element of developing a personal brand is having a website. Although having a significant social media presence is crucial, you do not own or have any control over the myriad of social platforms you use. Your website is a platform you own and control, and browsing it is frequently one of the first steps potential customers use on their way to becoming paying customers. So, take care of your website and it will take care of you. Nothing is more off-putting than a dated website that hasn't had a look-in by you for months or even years. Oh, the horror!

Even more dreadful are spelling mistakes. A huge no-no.

Get a professional to do your website and update it regularly.

First impressions matter a lot. Your target audience should be able to tell who you are and how you can help them when they land on your website. They ought to sense that they are in the correct place. Most new visitors will quit your website if this doesn't happen within a few seconds.

PASSIVE INCOME

"Passive income is the key to creating a life of financial freedom and abundance."

— ADAM SMITH

It isn't easy to be an entrepreneur when revenue sources frequently disappear. Having several different sources of income is crucial for this reason. While that sounds great, it can be challenging to put into practice.

Whether you're attempting to start a side business or are just looking to make a little extra money each month, passive income can be a workable approach to help generate additional cash flow. This is especially valid now that the economy is experiencing widespread inflation.

Passive income refers to money earned with minimal effort or active involvement. It is income that continues to flow in after an initial investment of time, money or effort, with little ongoing maintenance or participation required. Passive income streams typically do not rely on trading time for money, as is the case with a regular job.

When times are good, passive income can help you make more money. It can also help you to make ends meet if you suddenly lose your job, decide to take time off work, or if inflation keeps eating away at your purchasing power.

The average millionaire has seven sources of income, so you should build multiple income streams for yourself over the long term.

Here are the most common sources of income for millionaires, according to the IRS:

1) Dividend Income: Profits from stocks, mutual funds and exchange-traded funds (ETFs) kept in a brokerage account.

A firm can either reinvest its profits back into the company or spread some of them as dividends to its shareholders.

Dividends are typically paid once every three months and are subject to your marginal tax rate.

The more dividend-paying investments you purchase, the more money you can earn.

In my opinion, the best thing about dividends is that you can use them to buy more shares, which allows you to get more dividends (compound interest!).

It's a lovely thing!

2) Rental Income: Income from renting out real estate, including houses, apartments, offices and storage facilities.

Because all you need to do is collect the rent payments, rental income is relatively passive.

Of course, finding good tenants and managing the property will need some initial work. Still, once those tasks are completed, the money will flow in. The trick is finding perfect tenants. Easier said, but it is possible.

3) Royalties: Profits from selling inventions, books, etc.

You will receive royalties in exchange for using your intellectual property, such as patents, copyrights and trademarks.

If you create a brand-new form of a widget, for instance, you may sell the patent to a business that will compensate you with royalties for each time they utilize your invention.

Or, if you write a book, you can give a publisher your copyright in exchange for income from each sale.

Because you may make money without any effort once the product is selling, royalties are a fantastic source of passive income.

The same applies to music. If you make a hit record and are signed by a music label, you will get royalties on sales.

4) Interest Income: Profits from bonds, savings accounts, etc.

The money you make from lending money to another person is known as interest income.

For instance, if you have a savings account, the bank will provide interest on the money deposited.

Alternatively, the bond issuer will pay you interest if you invest in bonds.

Interest income is a fantastic kind of passive income since it allows you to make money without doing any labor!

The importance of passive income cannot be ignored. It is the single best way to create a life of freedom and choice as it reduces your dependency on a full-time job. Working a high income job or owning a high-flying businesses is great; but once you stop, so does the money.

> *"If you don't find a way to make money while you sleep, you will work until you die"*

— WARREN BUFFET

FINANCIAL MANAGEMENT FOR SMALL BUSINESSES

For your Small Business to Succeed, Cash Flow is Crucial.

One of the leading causes of company failure is a lack of capital. Suppose your cash is locked up in overdue or unpaid invoices and the client cannot pay their debts. In that case, even the most prosperous enterprises may quickly find themselves in trouble.

Cash flow can be one of the most challenging issues in the early stages of your business. There will be a lot of expenses when you're busy building your business but no clients or consumers to generate cash. Because of this, it's critical to think through your cash flow position at the outset and to have a short-term source of funds, such as savings or an overdraft, to cover expenses while you wait for the money to start coming in.

Additionally crucial is keeping a close check on cash flow for seasonal firms. You must carefully monitor and manage your cash flow if your revenue varies significantly throughout the year.

Track your Spending.

Do you keep track of your daily, weekly and monthly spending? If you don't keep an eye on your expenditure, you might be collecting debt that you can do without. Additionally, not keeping track of expenses might result in wasteful spending and overspending.

Numerous business owners maintain multiple accounts, including credit cards, savings and checkings accounts. To keep track of account balances, ensure you know the amount you withdraw or spend from each account.

Reduce Expenses while Boosting Sevenue.

Reducing spending and boosting income are two simple money management strategies that might be challenging to implement. If you're having trouble managing your company's finances, try finding strategies to boost revenue while reducing expenses.

To reduce costs, start by reviewing your spending. You may cut costs and eliminate extras by looking at your present expense categories and totals. Additionally, you can cut costs by looking around for new suppliers.

Offering discounts, advertising products through email marketing or social media adverts, introducing new products or services to sell, and setting up refer-a-friend and loyalty programs for small businesses are all effective ways to boost revenue.

KEY TAKEAWAYS

- **How to become an Entrepreneur - this burning flame is inside you. Otherwise, you wouldn't be thinking about it all the time!**
- **Creating a Business Plan -the most necessary document you will need. Without it, your business will be left floundering.**
- **Marketing your Business for great returns - no marketing means no one knows you're there. That's not sensible, is it?**
- **How to Build your Brand - you can have great fun doing this and you should be firmly entrenched in social media.**
- **Passive Income Streams to Build your Balance - getting dividend profits, rent from tenants and royalties are ways of getting ahead.**
- **Financial Management - one of the easiest ways for your business to go belly-up is not keeping track of cash flow. Keep your eyes on it all the time.**

COMING UP

How to land the job you've always wanted by guiding you in searching, planning and applying for your first job. Don't miss out on how to prepare for interviews.

TEEN TV

WHAT MAKES TIKTOK TICK FOR FINANCE WHIZ KIDS

Danika Miller, Personal Finance Reporter of The Simple Dollar, wanted to find out what makes TikTok tick for youngsters passionate about finance.

Taylor Price (@pricelesstay)
Taylor Price is a 20-year-old finance major with a passion for fintech. After a major spinal fusion surgery, Price was drawn away from her intended neurosurgery career and into finance. She is inspired by the innovation and freedom that the finance and investment world offers. Price started TAP Intuit, an educational platform aimed at teaching Generation Z about finance, after realizing many of her peers didn't know basics like a Roth IRA.

Q: How would you describe your particular angle and platform? Why do you think that has been successful?

Taylor Price: My angle has been formed around being a young woman in finance. As finance is still a male-dominated field, I was highly criticized in the beginning stages of my growth on TikTok for being a young female college student trying to educate my classmates. My platform has been successful because people can relate to me. I'm young, went through trauma with my spinal fusion, and I understand what it's like to know nothing about finance because I was there, too.

Q: Why do you enjoy sharing finance content on TikTok?

Taylor Price: I love sharing financial content on TikTok because that is where most Gen Z is and where school isn't. Only 6 out of 50 states require a personal finance class. My TikTok not only reaches the entire United States but the majority of the globe. Our vision statement at Team TAP is 'Learning today to build wealth tomorrow, showing the world what school never taught us.' At one point in our lives, we all go through the process of trying to build a budget, questioning credit scores, and so much more that our educational system lacks to prioritize.

Zaid Admani (@admani_explains)
Zaid Admani began day trading at 18 years old. Though he was planning a career in financial services, the Great Recession plagued his college years. Admani chose a steadier career course as a civil engineer. Yet, he continues to self-educate and maintain a passion for finance and credits. The platform allows him to explain concepts in the same way he taught himself without being bogged down by industry jargon.

Q: How is the TikTok finance space different from other platforms?

Zaid Admani: Content on TikTok is more discoverable and introduces finance to a group of people that might not have been interested before. Thousands of people never would have looked into finance content. Still, because it showed up in their TikTok feed, the content gets consumed - people discover that finance is interesting and not super complicated.

Q: How would you describe your particular angle and platform?

Zaid Admani: I try to explain things using skits and ordinary language. I watched a lot of CNBC as a kid. But I only understood half of the things the suits on CNBC would talk about. My angle is to simplify that. My language is loose. I curse a lot in the skits, but the point is to reduce the barrier for people to understand the business and finance world.

Q: What is your favorite or most surprising piece of financial advice?

Zaid Admani: I might get some heat for this, but I would look into investing a small portion of your portfolio into crypto. I'm most invested in Bitcoin and Ethereum. The potential long-term ROI is worth the risk. I'm not suggesting you invest all your money. But I currently have 10% of my portfolio in crypto.

One-Page Business Plan

The Business Opportunity
What problems are you resolving for customers?

Company Description
at does your company do? What product or service do you make or offer?

Team
Who is involved? Who is on your team Why are you the right person/people to build the business?

Industry Analysis
o are your competitors? What are some key factors that make those businesses successful?

Target Market
Who are your customers? Who are you selling to? What is your ideal customer and why would they purchase from you?

Timeline
hat needs to be done and when? What es first? What are the steps to launch the business?

Marketing
How will you reach your target audience? How will you convert them to customers? Where and how will you meet your audience?

Financial Summary
at is the cost structure of the business? hat are your revenue streams, fixed and riable costs? What are your short and long-term sales goals?

Funding
How much money do you need to start the business? Where will that money come from?

Basic Business Expenses

	Description	January	February	March	Total	Average
Product/ Service 1						
Product/ Service 2						
Total Cash In						

Fixed Expenses						

Variable Expenses						

Total Cash In						
Total Cash Out						
Net Cashflow						

LANDING YOUR VERY FIRST JOB

"If we all did the things we are capable of, we would literally astound ourselves"

— THOMAS EDISON

RESEARCHING CAREER OPTIONS

A brave new world opens when you land your first job and get your very first paycheck. You may feel elated and yet also intimidated. You've read so much about what you should do with your money you feel somewhat overwhelmed. Relax! It's something that most of us feel. With your paycheck safely tucked away, you can finally being to dream about the exciting path that lies ahead of you. Take your time. Your future awaits. It's not a race. It's an adventure.

Let's start by thinking about the type of work you would like to accomplish. For instance, if you are passionate about animals, ask if any area veterinarians are hiring. If working with children is more your style, inquire at your neighborhood

YMCA (many offer summer camps and after-school activities for kids) or childcare facilities.

Fast food joints and retail businesses rely on inexperienced staff and are open to training new hires. To assist with book storage, local libraries frequently hire teenagers. Teenagers can find various seasonal employment at amusement parks and summer programs.

Looking for Jobs

The easiest way is to go online! Type in what you're after, and you'll get the complete list of what is available. You'll be surprised at the many opportunities out there.

You can check online newspapers, community newsletters and online job boards. No doubt the Internet can often be overwhelming, so you can always visit the websites of prospective employers if you're interested in working at a specific company. Some post job opening advertisements directly on their websites or social media.

Alternatively, check the local stores in your neighborhood to see if any have job postings, such as in their window displays or on a bulletin board. You can also inquire with the manager or owner of these nearby businesses about any potential openings for entry-level personnel.

It's worth noting you may require a work permit: research your region and sector regulations to determine whether you must submit a permit application. These requirements frequently change depending on the field you wish to work in, where you live and how old you are.

For all kinds of teenage jobs, pay scales and much more, scour Monster online; it's a treasure trove of information!

Examples of Entry-Level Employment

Here are a few examples of jobs teens often apply for as their first introduction to the world of employment:

Camp counselor, car wash attendant, catering coordinator, childminder, coffee barista, customer service rep, delivery person, dishwasher, dog walker, fast food employee, gas station employee, gardener, house and office mover, janitor, junior referee, lifeguard, newspaper deliverer, payroll clerk, restaurant server, retailer, swim coach, theater usher, ticket seller, umpire, valet.

Internships, Part-Time Positions and Volunteer Work

An internship is a first job in a professional sector of employment. It is occasionally compensated mainly at the bottom of the pay scale and sometimes is unpaid. An internship's purpose is to gain knowledge in a particular subject while doing practical work in exchange for the experience.

People frequently associate internships with college students preparing to launch their careers. However, internship possibilities, like networking and trying out various job pathways, aren't just advantageous for college students. Teenagers can also use internships to figure out what they want to do with their lives and gain practical work experience.

High school students now have greater access to internships as remote work becomes increasingly prevalent. Many students can do internships like the ones below throughout the summer, on the weekends, or after school hours:

Childcare Assistance

Collaborating with other childcare professionals, a childcare assistant intern looks after and mentors young children from infancy through preschool under adult supervision. Additionally, interns could help with after-school events and recreation. Typically, this internship takes place over the summer or daily right after school.

A Student Teaching Assistant

Under the guidance of a lead teacher and any other adult aides or helpers, a teaching assistant intern assists in primary school classrooms. This position involves supervising students as they complete their homework, keeping watch for safe play at recess and providing support during class.

Production Assistant

Interns who work as production assistants produce audio and video content for businesses alongside production teams. Interns research the subjects the company intends to cover, take pictures and videos and edit the content they produce before it is distributed; this can also apply at radio stations.

Editorial

The Editor-in-Chief of a publication is typically the supervisor of an editorial intern who works with an editorial team. These interns might conduct research, make plans, edit both published and unpublished work, and help ensure the items' accuracy by fact-checking them. Employers typically look for strong writing and editing abilities when hiring students for these professions. Such internships may be conducted remotely or at a publication's office, such as a newspaper or magazine.

Social Media

Under the guidance of a social media manager, interns produce and post content for a company. The intern might investigate marketing strategies, assist in setting up social media campaigns and create pertinent graphics. Increasing followers and learning about marketing are often the objectives of this type of internship. Teenagers can complete these internships online throughout the academic year, however they might need to collaborate with their professors if the company only accepts applications during the school day.

Graphic Design

Interns in graphic design support teams in producing content for their clients. Editing photos, creating graphics and creating digital art that matches the client's brand and aesthetic are all included in this. These internships might need a design portfolio and graphic design software experience. Many of these internships are online, so students with access to computers at home can complete them all year round.

Marketing

A marketing intern assists this department of a business by conducting research, helping with ideas for campaigns and more. Students can select the industry they wish to learn about, such as book PR or retail outlets, since marketing is essential to numerous job disciplines. These internships might be local or remote, although hiring occurs most frequently in the summer when students can work alongside employees during the day.

Fashion

A fashion intern collaborates with marketing groups and designers to create apparel or accessories, plan photo shoots and research market trends. Interns learn all facets of fashion and successful sales techniques for the goods they design and produce. These internships are nearly always on-site, whether the employer is a big garment retailer or a small-town fashion designer looking for extra help. Nevertheless, fashion interns can work after school and on the weekends throughout the academic year.

Administrative

An intern collaborates with the office's administrators to ensure employees have a productive day. Typically, these interns acquire knowledge of the responsibilities of an administrative team, including taking calls, managing front-desk concerns and setting up appointments. Depending on their field of study, the intern might interact with various people, including businesspeople, tourists or patients. Students may only be hired over the summer or on weekends because employers usually prefer these interns on-site throughout the workweek.

Research

Interns in research collaborate with professionals conducting original research in their fields, such as scientists and historians. Several employment categories hire research interns in the sciences and the humanities, giving a candidate a wide range of options. The position's primary responsibilities include supporting lead researchers, carrying out tests or excavations and documenting findings in papers. Teenagers typically perform these internships on-site in the summer.

Business Development

A business development intern often assists a business manager with research, teamwork with the marketing and public relations departments, and developing original ideas for projects that would lift a company's profitability and visibility. Although employers rarely require prior experience, they want these interns to be detail-oriented and quick-thinking. High school students can participate in these internships in person for local firms throughout the summer, possibly on weekends or even during the school day.

Congressional Page

During legislative sessions, congressional page interns and regular congressional pages serve as the lawmakers' assistants. Distributing papers ahead of a session, providing Congresspeople with refreshments and information and delivering documents to authorities are all responsibilities. Legislators hire pages all year long, but they must work the entire day when Congress is in session, which can interfere with class schedules.

Curatorial Assistant

A curatorial assistant collaborates with a museum curator to ensure each exhibit runs appropriately. These interns could communicate with antique merchants or historical societies, assist with the design of exhibitions and keep track of display scheduling. Interns employed as curatorial assistants may work at either art or history museums, each of which has specific nuances that must be learned to thrive. Students looking for this kind of internship should contact their local museums, as they might offer summer or after-school activities.

Software Engineer Intern

An apprentice software engineer assists in developing or maintaining products while learning about coding languages from other software engineers and team leads. This internship may require you to research bug fixing, conduct data analysis and complete technical tasks. These internships are becoming more widely accessible to students year-round through remote possibilities as this profession grows in popularity. Sometimes, companies may insist on strong computer literacy and coding skills.

Online Jobs for Teens

Some online jobs can follow on nicely from a similar internship, as exhibited from the examples below:

Data Entry Clerk

National average hourly wage: $16.81

Data entry involves administrative labor, typing, voice recording and other processes to enter data into computers. Health care, finance, retail and transportation are just a few of the industries where data entry clerks might find employment.

Data entry tasks often call for quick and accurate typing abilities. Age restrictions vary depending on the business; in most companies, you must be 16 or 18 years old.

Freelance Graphic Designer

National average hourly wage: $19.88

Digital designs are created by graphic designers utilizing specialized tools and software. If you enjoy creating art online, consider finding a freelance graphic design job. The rates you charge, whether hourly or per job, are low, medium or high depending on your talent.

Technology and aesthetic skills are combined in this position. Thus, proficiency with graphic design software is a prerequisite. Creating projects for student organizations, nonprofits, political organizations, friends and family, and local institutions could be an excellent way to start building your portfolio.

Freelance Video Editor

National average hourly wage: $20.61

Numerous sectors employ video content providers, and independent editors are required to assimilate graphics, video and sound to convey a story.

Before applying for paid employment, it's recommended that you refine your video editing abilities and compile a portfolio. A freelancer's ability to maximize their earnings also depends on their ability to communicate with clients, manage their time to meet deadlines and be original and innovative.

Virtual Assistant

National average hourly wage: $21.93

A virtual assistant's primary responsibilities include various administrative activities for their clients. Tasks include taking calls, setting up appointments, reserving lodging, booking flights and managing client calendars.

Virtual assistants must be knowledgeable with the Internet, email and computer programs, as well as writing and oral communication, organization and time management skills.

Freelance Content Writer

National average hourly wage: $23.24

Content writers produce online blog posts and other webpage material for company websites. Writers of content are typically compensated per word or article. You can obtain employment as a freelance content writer if you have excellent writing, editing and grammar abilities.

Making an online portfolio of some of your greatest, error-free work is a fantastic idea. To succeed as a freelancer, you must also manage your time and communicate well.

Online Tutor

National average hourly wage: $24.79

Tutoring is one of the best-paying Internet professions for teenagers. While older students are typically the only ones who receive online tutoring, certain platforms let teenagers charge a fee to teach their classmates. You can teach foreign, non-native speakers language skills through online peer tutoring for a subject or course you have mastered.

Online tutoring positions frequently need teenagers to demonstrate their understanding of the subject or course by completing a test. Before a tutor can start working with other students, certain platforms may require them to be at least 18 years old and undergo training sessions. Since most platforms use video conferencing for sessions, most demand that tutors have a webcam.

Launch a YouTube Channel of your Own

Unlimited income potential!

To launch a YouTube channel, you must be an expert in video editing and computer usage. You must commit to consistently producing interesting videos on a regular basis to have a successful channel.

You must select your niche, such as a specific subject of interest of yours. You'll record and edit videos, produce thumbnails and titles, write descriptions, add YouTube tags and optimize them for profit. Spend time learning about YouTube algorithms and effective video-making techniques, such as selecting the appropriate equipment, producing videos of excellent quality or utilizing search engine optimization (SEO) strategies.

Market your channel on all social platforms. Remember, if people don't know about it, they won't watch it.

Online Polls and Reviews

Online surveys and reviews are among the simplest ways to get money online. It's vital to remember that the money you can make from surveys may be insignificant compared to other employment options. The typical survey income per hour might be between 40 cents and $2.

Online reviews involve evaluating content, such as a song, commercial, or TV show, intended to be published on a website or another platform. After reviewing the material, you can offer comments to assist businesses, artists and other organizations about how to revise their work to attract as much attention as possible.

Avoid giving out excessive amounts of personal information when taking surveys. Install anti-malware software and create an email account just for survey websites. Teens should first read the Terms of Service before signing up for an online survey platform. It's crucial to research the payment method because some websites pay with money while others offer gift cards for completing surveys.

CREATING AN IMPRESSIVE RÉSUMÉ

Use the steps below to make an impressive professional document if you are a teen writing your first résumé.

You must emphasize your talents and academic accomplishments in a professional document, regardless of whether you're seeking summer employment, a part-time position or a work placement.

If you are currently looking for your first job, you most likely have never had to prepare a résumé and are unsure where to begin; your résumé is crucial, but writing one doesn't have to be tough.

Although all résumés contain the same primary areas, customization is flexible if you want to highlight something; make use of the templates at the end of this chapter.

Generally speaking, you should contain the following sections:

Header: This will start with your name and move on to your contact information. Include your phone number, email and home address (or at least the town or city). Separately, make sure the email address you include is appropriate. It should be business-like, contain your full name and be devoid of nicknames and slurs (for example, cutiepatootie41@email.com).

Creating a fresh, professional email address for your job quest might be a good idea.

Summary: This is crucial since it functions as your sales presentation and is what employers will first notice. Here, you must briefly describe yourself, your top qualifications and talents, and the position you seek. Instead of discussing what you intend to get from the position, focus more on what you can provide.

Your educational background is listed here in reverse chronological order. In this part, you should list your college, high school and any independent courses you've attended, including online programs or workshops.

Skills: Since you may have little professional experience as a teenager, you must demonstrate your abilities in this part. Make sure your talents are appropriate for the position you're looking for. Use technical skills relevant to the position, such as software applications and programming languages, as well as transferrable qualities like communication and collaborative ability.

Experience: When listing previous positions and experience in the field, be careful to include contributions you made, such as assisting a teammate or going above and beyond your call of duty. Again, this section needs to be arranged in reverse chronological order with the most recent experience first. It is to be expected that as a teen, you're likely to have little working experience. Employers will understand. Make the most of what you have achieved personally, not corporately, and what this could bring to the role you'd like to apply for.

Additional Sections: You can include any more necessary and appropriate sections. You might include a section outlining your language abilities, the honors you have received, your interests and hobbies, musical skills or even your business endeavours.

MASTERING COVER LETTERS

A cover letter is a document, a few paragraphs long, that briefly describes your abilities for the job you're applying for and indicates your interest in the position. Your cover letter, along with your résumé, serves as a critical first impression to potential employers. As such, it must be crystal clear and make a compelling case for your appropriate experience (if you have some), abilities and education. While a cover letter is not required for every job you apply for, writing one can help you stand out from the competition and show the employer that you are genuinely interested in the role.

You should write a different cover letter for each job you apply for. For example, a cover letter for a barista job won't highlight the same skills that one for a sales associate position would. You should draft a basic cover letter highlighting your skills and abilities and tailor it to each job you apply for.

Like the structure of an essay, cover letters typically have three parts: an introduction, a body paragraph or two and a closing statement.

To begin creating a template, start by putting your details and contact information at the top of the page. It's a good idea to make this section clear and easy to read. This ensures the hiring manager has your contact information. For an emailed cover letter, include your email address, phone number and full name.

Make use of the template at the end of this chapter.

EXCELLING IN JOB INTERVIEWS

Do your Research!

Researching a company's past, core principles and mission statement in advance can make or break an interview. Throughout the interview, you can use your research to show that you are a team player with the interests of the company's overall values in mind.

According to Amy Marschall, a psychologist who frequently helps young people looking for jobs and the author of a mental health blog, this preparation allows you to analyze the situation carefully. "It looks good if you know things about the position as well as the company, and this helps you know if it's a job you want," adds the expert.

Google the business, read through several pages on their website (such as the "About" page or mission statement, along with blog posts that demonstrate their values). Use social media to see what current or former employees are saying about it; check out their Muse profile (if they have one) to get a behind-the-scenes look at company culture. Spending time at the actual business (such as a restaurant or grocery store) to get a feel for its operations is an excellent research method too.

You can also search for any company-related news to stay current on any recent good and bad happenings. For instance, you should read the restaurant chain's recent announcement of a brand-new seasonal menu and bring it up in your interview.

Talk Confidently about Yourself.

Prepare to talk about yourself. This is not an ego trip, as a vital part of the interview, you needn't feel overly humble or shy. You are telling your story, which is very valid, and the way you conduct yourself will tell the interviewer a lot about your suitability. Gauge the situation - add a little humor, too, if it feels appropriate.

Practice this thoroughly and present it to your parents. Tell it straight, like you are with the interviewer. Many people fall apart during this section; maybe you don't like talking about yourself. You blush, and stammer, and the interviewer turns off. Get confidence. You are very important. Prove it.

Also, don't rock up to the interview in ripped jeans. You may think they're swell, but your interviewer will not. Always dress conservatively.

The Phone Interview

The first step in the employment process is frequently a phone interview with a recruiter. This is a very crucial aspect of your employment hunt, as the recruiter will question your history, abilities and experience to determine whether they are relevant to the open position.

They can also check if your personality fits the company's culture. If everything goes as planned, the recruiter will advance you to the next level. But progress is unlikely if they leave with a negative or incomplete opinion of you.

The next round of the interview procedure is also frequently done over the phone. You will probably speak with the recruiting manager or another hiring team member during this step. As the interviewer has a stronger understanding of the vacant position and the qualifications necessary for success, this interview is typically more in-depth than the phone screening.

These two interviews typically last 30 minutes each. Consider phone interviews as a time to highlight your top reasons for applying for the position and the firm, as well as your strengths and qualifications.

Since it's only your voice at play here (meaning there are no cues from your body language to assist), sound warm, inviting and professional; confident but friendly.

The Video Interview

You're undoubtedly already familiar with the fundamentals of preparing for a video interview: make sure your mic is on, choose a peaceful and well-kept spot, and put on some jeans (not ripped!). Let's explore how you can take your digital interviewing abilities to the next level, as more and more employers are using Google Hangout, Zoom, or Meet interviews, meaning other job seekers are familiar with the fundamentals.

You can minimize technical issues by practising your setup beforehand using the same platform, internet connection, and hardware you'll use during your interview. Invite a friend to ensure you can hear, be heard and be seen during a video chat. Spend some time learning the program's fundamentals and ensuring you understand how to mute and unmute your microphone.

The firm and your interviewer control the environment for an in-person interview but not for a video interview. You can make sure your physical shot makes a favorable impression, for example if you are using a phone, keep it upright in a phone stand rather than holding it in your hand.

Set up in a peaceful location in front of the most neutral backdrop you can find, such as a blank wall or a space devoid of distracting clutter or décor. If this isn't an option, consider blurring your background. Ensure that you have good lighting —natural light is preferred—and the lighting source is behind your computer or phone, not behind you.

If you have trouble finding a room in your house with sufficient natural lighting, consider spending money on a selfie ring light that fits around the camera of your laptop or phone.

Check to see whether anything in your shot reflects or emits a glare that can distract your interviewer before deciding on your attire and location. The most common offenders are typically watches, jewelry or spectacles; the solution may be as simple as taking away one piece.

Naturally, not everyone can remove their spectacles before an interview. To minimize the glare as much as you can, try some of these techniques:

- Instead of aiming your lamp at yourself, direct it to bounce off the wall behind your desk.
- Consider changing or removing your lampshade.
- Adjust the height of your laptop's display or the stand for your phone.

In a video interview, most people are more concerned with how they appear than how they speak. Ask the person you are practicing with if any of these things make it more difficult for them to hear or understand you. As you practice, pay attention to how quickly you speak, how you pause and the tone and pitch of your voice.

It could be tempting to have a lot of information in front of you for a video interview, but take care. Keep only a few brief notes in front of you and try to only sometimes look at them. Highlight in your notes essential data and make them short passages, not whole solutions. You must not come over like you're reading from a script.

Similarly, close any auxiliary windows and irrelevant tabs to prepare your computer. Additionally, if you want to share a screen during your interview to display a portfolio or something similar, make sure it is prepared and open in a window that is minimized but still easy to access.

To be On Time is to be Late

You wouldn't arrive at the location of an interview at 3 PM if that is your scheduled meeting time, or even at 2:59 PM, so you shouldn't do it for a video interview.

Often, online meeting platforms require an invitee to be "let in" to the virtual space by the host. By joining the video interview early, say at least 5 minutes, this gives your interviewer the opportunity to recognise your organisation, time-keeping and professionalism. They may not be ready themselves, as there is always the possibility they are interviewing another candidate before you, so why not take this opportunity to ready yourself with a deep breath and a sip of water.

Use your Face to Demonstrate your Engagement

In each interaction, nonverbal cues are crucial. However, many ways we typically convey nonverbal cues—such as eye contact, body language and subtle murmurs of agreement—are restricted while doing a video interview. Therefore, we must rely more on what is still available: facial expressions, for example raising your eyebrows, smiling and nodding your head. Your interviewer shouldn't have to question whether you're still connected because you're being too static.

Let the other Speaker Finish their Sentence.

This is sound advice for life in general, but on a video chat, be aware that responding too fast will silence the other person's mic and completely cut them off, making you appear impolite even if you weren't trying to be. Additionally, due to Internet lag, it's not always clear if someone is finished speaking or merely pausing. Therefore, wait until you believe your interviewer has finished before responding. If you struggle with this, practice shutting off your microphone while the other person is speaking; this will require you to allow them a little more time to finish their sentence.

Important Last Words

Imagine the following scenario:

Congratulations! You have successfully passed the first round of phone interviews. You prepared everything for the ideal video interview, including the attire, environment and lighting. Five minutes into the interview, your voice and image drift out of sync, everything freezes and the video abruptly ends. You can contact your interviewer by phone, but you are left to worry if they can get past the technical difficulties and get to know the real you.

It's important to remember: these things happen. Although there is no way to ensure the scenario above won't occur, here are four things you can do to minimize the chances:

1. Make sure you have enough bandwidth.
2. Ask those in the house to stay off the Wi-Fi during your interview.
3. Do a trial run at the same time of day your interview is scheduled.
4. Close all the other open apps and restart your computer.

Good luck!

KEY TAKEAWAYS

- **How to Look for Jobs – going online is your first port of call. Don't become overwhelmed. Take your time and scour what's waiting for you.**
- **Finding Available Work – we've shown you a snippet of what's available, so start by reading, calling companies and making notes.**
- **How to Create a Great CV and Cover Letter – very important! This is usually the first time that people will learn about you. If it looks sloppy, you won't get that interview.**
- **How to Excel in Job Interviews – some thrive under stress, while others fall apart at this crucial part of your budding career.**
- **Mastering the Art of Video Interviews - today, it's all about the video interview, and it is an art! Learn to become a true professional at it.**

COMING UP

How to build a formidable financial foundation by creating savings and investing accounts.

TEEN TV

RUSSELL'S VIDEO DISASTER TURNED FABULOUS

Russell thought he had it all together for his Google Meet video call with an HR department about the job he was applying for. "Please," he thought, "I've done this so often. What could go wrong?" What could go wrong, indeed...

He had chosen, for whatever reason, to use one of the pool chairs, which are not the sturdiest at the best of times. While going well initially, Russell became slightly over-confident.

During his interview, he leaned backwards to adjust a standing light behind him. Can you guess what happened? That's right, the chair fell backwards, taking Russell along with it.

In one fell swoop, he tumbled over, releasing a high pitched squeal as he went, startling the interviewer, Sally. Worse still, having only prepared his top half for camera, Russel flashed the perfect view of his stripy briefs and odd socks as he went head over heels!

Sally fell apart; she was laughing so much she was crying. A devastated Russell pulled himself and the chair up. He faced the executioner with as much bravado as he could manage.

"I'm so sorry," he said. "I don't know what to say."
It didn't matter what he said because Sally, along with her

assistant Paul watching from the side, were falling about, unable to talk back.

"If you'd like to end this now, that's fine," stammered Russell. Sally was just able to shake her head; she believed the interview had to go on. Russell could only look on in abject misery.

Eventually, Sally pulled herself together, tears streaming down her cheeks, and asked him if he had learned his lesson.

Russell could merely nod his head.

To his surprise, she then asked him if he would like to come in for a physical interview at their offices.

Russell couldn't believe his ears!

"You have brightened our day," said Sally. "And the great thing is we are recording this, so we can play it repeatedly when we feel down." Russell blushed furiously.

"Don't worry," said Sally. "The other candidates were terribly dull. You pulled yourself together very well -that's a big plus. Oh, and, by the way, when you come in, wear some pants, okay?"

[Your Name], High School Student

123 My Address, My Town, City, State, Zip, [0123]456-789, abc@gmail.com

PROFILE	Briefly summarise your background and the role you are looking for. Maybe describe yourself in a couple of short sentences, highlighting the attributes that you think are most suitable for the job.
EDUCATION [Years Studied]	[Your School] • GPA • Subjects Studied • Awards
EXTRA-CURRICULAR ACTIVITIES [Dates]	Mention any activities you do outside of school to demonstrate extra skills, interests and commitments. This could include volunteering, playing in a band or community service. Mention what skills you've learned and what responsibilities you had. Employers want to see more than just your academic achievements, so this is the place to make yourself stand out as a well-rounded, adaptable person.
EMPLOYMENT HISTORY [Dates]	[Job Position] Outline your role in the job, and again, mention the skills you learned and your responsibilities. You could also say how you handled a challenging situation or went the extra mile to help someone.
SKILLS	Mention your strengths that may be relevant to the job. You might be great at teamwork and communication or being organized. Staying calm in stressful situations or computing are also examples.
HOBBIES	What makes you unique? Are you great at sports, music or photography, for example?
REFERENCES	You may choose to put a reference here or leave "references available on request". This is so a potential employer can talk to someone, like an old boss or teacher, to find out if what you have said here is true.

[Your Name]
High School Student

23 My Address, My Town, City, State, Zip,
[0123]456-789, abc@gmail.com

PROFILE

I am a friendly, hard-working High School
Student looking for part-time and holiday
work in retail. I have a year of customer
service experience working as a server in a
local restaurant. There, I learned how to work
in a team and manage busy situations calmly.

EXPERIENCE

Server 2021 - 2022
Ben's Burgers

Babysitting 2021 - 2022
Babysitting for local families

SKILLS

- Customer service
- Teamwork and communication
- Cleaning and maintaining equipment
- Following the procedures and directions of
  the manager

TRAINING

Barista Training Course
Captain Coffee Basic Barista Course - 2022

EDUCATION

2022 - High School Student
Green Park High School - Grade 11 (current)
Grades so far achieved - SATs, ACTs or AP

AWARDS

Gold with Honours - 2022
Green Park High School

Gold Academic Award - 2021
Green Park High School

VOLUNTEERING

'Shelter' Homeless Charity 2022
Working late shifts helping those in need

Woofers Dog Shelter - 2021

INTERESTS

I play piano and French horn in the local
brass band and enjoy photography and
cycling.

Probationary Drivers Licence

(Your Name) Cover Letter

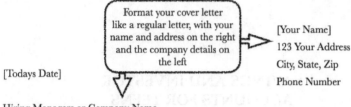
Format your cover letter like a regular letter, with your name and address on the right and the company details on the left

[Your Name]
123 Your Address
City, State, Zip
Phone Number

[Todays Date]

Hiring Managers or Company Name
Company Address
City, State, Zip

Introduce yourself and the role you are applying for

Dear [Mr/Mrs/Ms] [Hiring Managers Name/Sir/Madam],

My name is [name], I am a graduating student at [High School] School and I am writing with keen interest to apply for the [position] role on your website. My academic skills, qualifications and career goals align with the objectives of the [internship/job], making me a great candidate for the role.

In addition to my business classes, which cover a broad range of financial topics [such as], I served as secretary of the Student Council and volunteered at a local business, helping their accounts department. There, I learned the fundamentals of business finance and took on increasing responsibility which demonstrates my eagerness to learn.

Summarise your relevant skills and experience, tell the reader why you are interesting and suitable for the role

I have developed great teamwork and communication skills through involvement in the school hockey team and the brass band. This has given me great confidence in meeting new people and working successfully in a group, which is vital for this position.

I've attached my résumé, which further details my skills and qualifications. Please don't hesitate to contact me if you would like to speak further. Thank you for your time and consideration and I hope to hear from you soon.

Sincerely yours,

Use 'sincerely' if you know the name of the recipient. Use 'yours truly' if you do not.

Thank the reader for taking the time to read your application and sign off with yours 'truly' or 'faithfully'

Your Name

6

SAVINGS AND INVESTOR ACCOUNTS FOR TEENS

"Rule No.1 is never lose money. Rule No.2 is never forget rule number one."

— WARREN BUFFETT

WHAT TO INVEST IN AS A TEENAGER?

Teenagers are getting more financially savvy, yet many still lack investing know-how. It's a critical knowledge gap this book aims to close by enlightening and helping young investors choose what's right for them as individuals.

Fidelity's (2022) 'Teens and Money Study' demonstrated that 55% of those they asked said 'investing is too confusing'. According to 47%, investing feels 'out of reach' or 'takes too much time/attention'. Furthermore, 42% believe teenagers cannot trade stocks, period.

The fact that minors cannot open brokerage accounts is a significant hinderance. There are few options for teens, most requiring a parent or custodian to approve everything.

Although most teenagers have yet to dip a toe in the water, many identified investing as an eventual goal (91% of them told Fidelity they planned to do so).

So, while 72% of respondents claim to have no experience trading equities or ETFs, 50% *had* used a payment app, 49% had opened a bank account and 39% are actively seeking employment.

So, let's clear up any confusion about the best investments for teenagers *today*. To assist in clarifying any misconceptions you might have, we'll also examine the many sorts of accounts teens can use to get started and address a few other frequently-asked questions.

The Best Investments for Under 18's

Let's delve into some popular, typically easy-to-access assets that teenagers can buy in their investment accounts or that parents can hold for their teens until they legally reach 'adulthood':

Stocks

For various reasons, stocks are among the finest investments for teenagers. Benefits include:

- Better ROI rates in comparison to almost every other asset class.
- They are available for a variety of investment account types.

Stocks of businesses that teenagers actually engage with always make the best investments as they are more likely to be genuinely interested in following the company's development.

You can hold stocks individually, through mutual funds or ETFs.

Mutual Funds

Although stocks are fantastic, if you focus your investment funds on a small number of them, you run a significant chance of losing everything. Consider this: businesses collapse, and when they do, their stock prices may decrease to nothing. Suppose you have $10,000 spread evenly among only four stocks and one collapses. In that case, your entire investment portfolio has lost 25% of its value. Mutual funds are recommended because it takes the pressure off teens assuming this much risk.

Mutual funds are collections of different assets, usually stocks, bonds, or a mix of the two. By investing in a mutual fund, you buy into a diverse portfolio of stocks that a mutual fund may have, which could number in the dozens or even hundreds; this diversification helps lower risk.

There are several strategies to diversify, such as by holding:

- Different equities in one market segment (like technology).
- Mixed equities across several sectors.
- Multiple stocks in multiple nations.
- Various assets such as shares, bonds and commodities like gold or oil.

Several investment accounts, such as IRAs, 529 plans and education savings accounts (ESAs), allow you to keep mutual funds. If you're unfamiliar with these accounts, don't worry, they're covered later in this chapter.

Exchange-Traded Funds

As we covered in Chapter 3, ETFs are the cousin of mutual funds and are worth getting acquainted with.

They often maintain a broad portfolio of stocks, bonds and other investments; ETFs are comparable to mutual funds in this regard. However, ETFs have grown significantly in popularity over the past few decades because of how they differ from conventional funds.

Most ETFs are index funds, unlike their mutual fund cousins, which are mainly actively managed. As a result, ETFs typically have substantially lower average prices. Even actively managed ETFs can be less expensive than comparable mutual funds, making them a financially realistic starting point for teens.

In addition, ETFs offer some tax benefits that enhance their performance by allowing you to see their holdings on any given day (as opposed to merely a quarterly snapshot for mutual fund holdings).

Bonds

Compared to stocks, bonds typically offer smaller returns but lower risks. A bond is essentially a loan you give to some kind of entity, usually a business or a government division. The issuing company guarantees to repay you within the specified time frame, plus interest, typically every six months.

Teenagers (and the vast majority of investors, for that matter) are better suited to purchasing bonds through mutual funds and ETFs because most bonds are challenging to research and buy on their own. You can diversify by purchasing exposure to hundreds or even thousands of bonds.

A savings bond is one example that is simpler for most people to purchase on their own. You can now purchase savings bonds by going to TreasuryDirect.gov. In contrast to most other bonds, when you redeem the bond, the principal (your initial investment) and interest are paid all at once.

Both Series EE and Series I savings bonds are readily available. The US Treasury promises that if you hold Series EE bonds for 20 years, your investment will at least double. Series I savings bonds offer both a fixed interest rate and an inflation-adjusted interest rate determined twice a year to protect your money from inflation.

A teen can only obtain a savings bond as a gift from an adult, as they can only be bought by people at least 24 years old.

High-Yield Savings Accounts

As you might expect from the name, high-yield savings accounts offer substantially greater interest rates than conventional savings accounts (typically by 20 - 25x greater!).

An ATM card is typically provided with the account, allowing unlimited deposits and withdrawals.

Most banks provide Federal Deposit Insurance Corporation (FDIC) insurance of up to $250,000 per account, so high-yield savings accounts are one of the safest methods to invest your money.

The negative? Yields on savings accounts aren't assured. Savings rates change along with interest rates over time as they go up and down. Additionally, while high-yield accounts offer rates significantly greater than the typical savings accounts, they often have considerably smaller upside potential than stocks, bonds and other products.

High-yield savings accounts offer those wanting to earn a little additional money the advantage that they can withdraw their funds at any time, which teens may need.

Certificates of Deposit

As we touched on also in Chapter 3, a CD is a loan to a bank for a predetermined period, they are a longer-term commitment in contrast to savings accounts.

With CDs, you'll generally receive a greater rate than with high-yield savings accounts, but you'll pay a penalty if you withdraw your money early. Therefore, a CD is the best option for teenagers who don't need their money immediately but will at a specific time and want to earn a little additional income while waiting.

Resources

When you get off to the correct start, learning about investing, spending and saving early can pay off greatly. Fidelity's Dedicated Youth Learning Center is available to parents and teens. It is stocked with resources created especially to assist teens in developing wise financial practices.

For example the Fidelity® Youth Account; a brokerage account controlled by teenagers aged 13 to 17 is one tool that can assist you in making that transition and beginning your investing adventure. You can start investing by trading most American equities, ETFs, and Fidelity mutual funds in your brokerage account.

You will also receive a free debit card with no monthly fees, account fees, minimum balance requirements, or domestic ATM fees. You may manage your money and utilize it anytime you need to by using this free teen debit card.

Controls that Parents Need and Want

For a teen to open a Fidelity® Youth Account, a parent or guardian must either already have one themselves or register for one with the company. Opening an account is simple, as there are no minimums or account fees for new Fidelity® members.

To keep an eye on your activity, parents and guardians can monitor debit card transactions done in the account and follow monthly bills and trade confirmations online.

Consider opening a Fidelity® Youth Account with your parents if you are interested in learning about investing. Your needs are considered when creating the account, enabling you to start building for the future and becoming financially independent.

Investment Accounts for Teens: Which Assets Should You Put in Each?

Here are the most popular types of accounts for teen investors (this includes accounts ultimately are controlled by a parent or custodian, however still allows teens to operate them and give their input):

1. Joint Brokerage Account

When you create an individual brokerage account for yourself, the account title will list your name as the owner. On the other hand, if you choose to open a brokerage account with two or more people, this is a joint brokerage account where you share ownership.

Spouses frequently form brokerage accounts, but they can also be opened by two or more people who have similar financial objectives (such as business partners or unmarried partners). Family members can also open joint brokerage accounts (for example, a father and son).

When a parent and teen possess a brokerage account jointly, they can decide what to buy and sell together. Setting one up is simple: many teen investing applications can facilitate this.

Financial assets you can hold within a joint brokerage account:

- Stocks
- Bonds
- ETFs
- Mutual funds
- Cash

2. Custodial Account

Custodial accounts are frequently used by parents who want to make investments and manage money on their children's behalf. The beneficiary owns the funds in the account, which the custodian manages. Still, a parent can involve their teen by talking to them about (or even having them help with) investment decisions in the account.

The assets stored in the custodial account revert to the owner's authority when the child or teen reaches the age of maturity, typically 18 or 21, but can occasionally be as old as 25. The custodial brokerage account owner is permitted to withdraw funds for any purpose.

There are two custodial accounts: UGMA (Uniform Gifts to Minors Act) and UTMA (Uniform Transfers to Minors Act). The most significant difference between them is that UGMA accounts can be used to keep purely *financial* assets. UTMA accounts can store financial assets and any additional type of asset, such as real estate or cars.

You may keep the following financial assets in a custodial account:

- Stocks
- Bonds
- Mutual Funds
- ETFs
- Cash Annuities
- Term Life Insurance

3. Individual Retirement Accounts (IRAs) Under Custodianship

You can use tax-efficient IRAs to set aside earned money for retirement savings. There are two main types of these accounts:

Traditional IRA: By contributing to a Traditional IRA, you can obtain a tax benefit immediately whilst saving pretax money that will appreciate over time. When you later withdraw money, though, taxes will be due.

Roth IRA: A Roth IRA enables you to make investments with post-tax money. Your contributions can not only grow tax-free, if you deposit to this tax-advantaged savings account, you may also make tax-free withdrawals.

The annual contribution limit cannot exceed your earned income. It was capped at $6,500 in 2023, and if you're 50 or older, the limit is $7,500.

For teens under 18, the IRA must be custodial, which implies an adult is in charge. By making regular retirement contributions teenagers can realize more upside potential through compounding returns. Even better, a teen doesn't *have* to pay for the money; free to keep their earnings, they can ask loved ones to contribute to their IRA up to the amount of their earned income in the year of the contribution.

When you put money into an IRA, you are using various investment techniques to safeguard your financial future. Access to assets outside standard classes is also provided by IRAs.

Among the financial resources you may keep in an IRA:

- Stocks
- Bonds
- ETFs
- Mutual Funds
- Cash Alternatives

Key Considerations

Savings accounts are becoming more competitive because of rising interest rates.

Online banks provide higher interest rates on high-yield savings accounts than traditional brick-and-mortar banks.

Despite offering lower interest rates, several savings account types may be better suited for various financial objectives due to their different deposit and withdrawal terms and conditions.

When selecting a savings account, compare fees, minimum balance requirements, customer service, convenience and interest rates.

Savings Accounts that Pay Interest

Along with savings accounts for investments, there are numerous types of savings accounts simply for regular deposits you wish to make after receiving money for your birthday from Grandma, for example.

However, it's crucial to remember that looking for a savings plan based solely on greater interest rates isn't always the best course of action. Each different type can help with various monetary objectives.

To determine which is right for you, weigh up all your options and consider speaking with a reputable financial counselor.

Standard Savings Accounts

The interest rates on traditional savings accounts are usually the lowest, but they also have the lowest fees and can offer the most convenience. These are provided by conventional banks and other financial organizations with physical locations and branches.

A standard savings account is ideal for those prioritizing easy access to their funds over greater interest rates. They are the choice for those who desire to increase their money over the long term or save money for a particular objective, such as a trip or a large purchase, that they can make instant withdrawals from.

Money Market Accounts

While incorporating features from both checking and savings accounts, money market accounts typically offer higher interest rates than standard savings accounts. One important thing to note; you usually need to maintain a minimum amount in a money market account.

They enable you to earn a better return than with a conventional savings account while saving for a particular objective — like purchasing a home or setting up a college fund — while still having access to your money.

Accounts with High Yields

Online banks and online credit unions generally provide high-yield savings accounts. These have interest rates far greater than money market accounts.

A high-yield savings account is ideal for people who want to accumulate short-term funds. These could be useful for saving for a big purchase or an emergency fund.

An account with a high return can quickly accumulate money thanks to compound interest. However, because it is variable, the rate of building your savings will slow down if interest rates do.

Deposit Certificates

High-yield savings accounts often offer lower interest rates than CDs, however there is a fee for early withdrawals.

Over the CD's term, the interest rate is fixed and won't go down or change. Additionally, CDs bought through FDIC- or NCUA-insured institutions are covered up to a maximum of $250,000 per account holder.

CDs also use compound interest to compare the actual yearly return. Look at the APY (Annual Percentage Yield); the interest rate on a CD is typically higher the longer its term of maturity.

These accounts are a choice to consider if you want your savings to grow but don't need immediate access to your funds.

· · ·

A Fixed Annuity

The highest interest rates are often seen in fixed annuities. You can use these insurance contracts to save for retirement or as a component of your total retirement strategy.

As their self-explanatory name suggests, they have a fixed rate that is guaranteed for the entire annuity and can be set up to give you a consistent income stream once you retire. Note that they are unsuitable for short-term goals.

529 Plan

A 529 plan is a savings plan with tax advantages intended to assist in covering educational expenses.

This college savings plan is excellent for parents seeking to set aside funds for their child's higher education, as the funds allocated to the account experience tax-free growth, provided they are utilized for qualified educational expenses.

Contributed funds are subsequently invested into a predetermined (by the account holder) array of investment options; typically mutual funds.

The following are the best-ranked 529 plans according to Forbes:

- New York's 529 College Savings Program – Direct Plan
- U.Fund College Investing Plan (Massachusetts)
- UNIQUE College Investing Plan (New Hampshire)
- Bright Start Direct-Sold College Savings Program (Illinois)
- Ohio's 529 Plan, CollegeAdvantage – Direct Plan
- Oregon College Savings Plan

All the above can be frightening for teens (and adults), but stick with it and find out more online or from a professional financial adviser if you think you need additional info. If you are a parent planning for your teen's financial future, starting early could be their saving grace.

KEY TAKEAWAYS

- **The Best Investments for Under 18s - think easy access! Is there a company you'd be genuinely interested in keeping up with their stock prices? Keep the pressure of risk at bay by contemplating mutual funds and don't forget those tax benefits of ETFs!**
- **Parental Controls - a Fidelity® Youth Account is a simple and safe account for teens but nosey parents can still keep a keen eye on their transactional activity.**
- **Savings Accounts for Investments - joint brokerage accounts, custodial accounts and IRAs remain the most popular types of accounts for teen investors.**
- **Choosing a Savings Account in Relation to Interest Rates - remember, just because a savings plan has the highest interest rate doesn't always guarantee it to be the best option for Grandma's birthday check! Consider deposit limits, withdrawal terms and conditions and tax advantages.**

CONCLUSION

⑤

Individuals invest to earn a profit and do so by utilising the various investment categories, or "asset classes," each providing a distinct kind of return. Investors might get dividends from shares, interest from cash or bonds, rent from real estate or capital gains when they sell an asset.

If you saw the above text at the beginning of this book, you may well have gone, "Huh?". Hopefully, after carefully examining all the explanations in this guide, you will now have a completely different response. This book has aimed to make even the most detailed descriptions, complex examples and challenging fiscal dynamics easy to follow.

Growing up, I knew I wanted to make a lot of money. I had big plans for starting businesses and investing, but teaching myself the fundamentals I've now presented in this book was frustrating, confusing and slow. How could I get ahead of the game when I lacked even the most basic knowledge of taxes and budgeting? I was only learning this critical information as and when I needed to, by which time it was too late. It should not be that way!

The problem was, and still is, universal; the education system fails to enlighten us with the knowledge we *all* need. As such, I wanted to make this the perfect vehicle for those starting on the road to riches. I hope you will have been inspired by what you found on these pages.

Here, then, is a brief recap (for those who start at the conclusion before going to the front!) to firmly imbed what you've read:

Chapter One helped you to understand the real value of money. Budget basics and how to set financial goals were explored. Learning key fiscal terminologies was introduced.

In **Chapter Two**, we set out to help readers you understand the importance of savings, banking, taxes and insurance.

Chapter Three introduced the exciting world of investments, with you becoming accustomed to stocks, bonds, shares, mutual funds and property.

In **Chapter Four**, strategies were planned for teenage entrepreneurs. Readers learned how to create business ideas and opportunities and how to market and sell their products to the desired audience.

Chapter Five focused on the world of employment, guiding readers on searching, planning and applying for that dream job. It examined how to create a great CV and cover letter – and, importantly, how to prepare for interviews (with an emphasis on video interviews).

Chapter Six, our bonus chapter, introduced readers to various savings and investment accounts, their individual suitability, how to open them and, importantly, how to use them!

Remember, it's great practise to find yourself a financial planner recommended by a trusted friend; such a person will be vital for your growth in the years ahead as you are able to take on more financial responsibility. Also, to keep abreast of what's happening in the financial arena by going online.

There are plenty of great sites; feel free to make use of our reference guide at the end of the book.

For me, money matters are the stuff that dreams are made of.

If you enjoyed this book, I trust they will be your dreams, too.

I WOULD LOVE TO HEAR FROM YOU!

$

I't's through your support and reviews that my book is able to reach the hands of other teens too. Please kindly leave a review on Amazon, all it takes is 60 seconds to make a difference!

GLOSSARY OF FINANCIAL TERMS

$$\text{(\$)}$$

A
DJUSTABLE-RATE MORTGAGE (ARM)
A mortgage that permits the lender to adjust the interest rate periodically based on changes in a specified index.

Administered Rate

An interest rate set directly rather than being influenced by the market forces of supply and demand.

Annual Percentage Rate (APR)

APR is the cost you pay each month to borrow fees from the bank if you do not pay your credit card balance back in full. It is a variable percentage calculated at a monthly rate, however is represented as an annual rate as a way of standardising comparison figures across credit card companies.

Annuity

A series of fixed payments of the same amount paid at regular intervals (i.e., every week, month, or pay period) over a specified period.

Appreciation

An increase in value. Currency appreciation is an increase in the value of one currency relative to another.

Asset

A resource with economic value that an individual, corporation, or country owns with the expectation that it will provide future benefits.

Assets Under Management (AUM)

Refers to the total market value of all the financial assets (such as stocks, bonds, cash, and other investments) that a financial institution, investment firm, or individual manages on behalf of their clients.

Asset Value

One measure used by investors to calculate the worth of a company. A company's debts are usually deducted to calculate a net asset value, also known as book value.

Automatic Transfer

An online payment automatically deducted from the account balance on a recurring basis.

Bank Statement

A statement given to account holders by a bank or credit union to inform them of all transactions they made during a statement period. These statements are sent regularly via mail or are accessible via online banking.

Balance-Sheet

In accounting, this is a statement of the assets and liabilities of a business. It must 'balance'; in the sense that assets equal liabilities. The assets, such as cash, equipment or inventory, are being used in the business; the liabilities show how those assets were funded, whether in the form of loans (owed to creditors) or equity (owed to shareholders).

Blockchain

A distributed ledger used to make a digital record of the ownership of assets, in particular cryptocurrencies.

Bonds

IOUs issued by a borrower typically promising repayment of the money on a set date (maturity) with regular interest payments during the bond's life. The riskier the issue, the higher the bond's interest rate (or yield). Governments issue bonds to cover the gap between the amount they receive in taxes and the amount they spend. Companies issue bonds to finance investment programs.

Bond Yield

The average return from owning a bond depends on the price paid for the bond, its coupon payments and time to maturity.

Budget

An itemized summary of probable income and expenses for a given period. A budget is a plan for managing income, spending, and saving during a given period.

Capital Gains

A profit from the sale of financial investments that increase in value.

Cash Flow

Income (dollars coming in, usually from working) minus expenses (dollars going out to buy goods and services).

Certificate of Deposit (CD)

A savings alternative in which money is left on deposit for a stated period to earn a specific interest rate.

Check-Cashing Services

Businesses that provide services such as cashing all kinds of checks, including payroll, insurance, tax refund, settlement and government and Social Security payments. These businesses may also provide other services like payday loans, money orders and money wires.

Checking Account

An account held at a financial institution in which account owners deposit funds. Account owners can write checks on their accounts and use ATM or debit cards to access funds.

Collateral (Elementary)

Something of value that a bank can keep if a borrower fails to repay a loan.

Comprehensive insurance

Vehicle insurance that provides coverage for theft or damage from incidents, not including a collision.

Compound Interest

Interest compounded on the sum of the original amount plus accrued interest.

Consumer Price Index (CPI)

A measure of the average change in prices over a period of time, paid by consumers for goods and services, for example food or rent. It is commonly used to give an indication as to the rate of inflation.

Creditor

A person, financial institution or other business that lends money.

Credit Score (also see FICO Credit Score)

A number based on information in a credit report, which indicates a person's credit risk. The higher the score, the better.

Cryptocurrency

Digitally (and mostly, privately) created Tokens. Ownership and transfer are recorded in a distributed ledger called the blockchain. Its highly volatile values make it difficult to be a store of value or a medium of exchange.

Debit Card

A plastic card similar to a credit card that allows money to be withdrawn or payments made directly from the holder's bank account. Unlike a credit card, payments and withdrawals are instant, leaving the bank account immediately.

Debtor

A person or organization that owes an amount of money.

Default

A failure to meet financial obligations, such as a when a borrower misses or stops making loan payments, for example, on a mortgage. For example, 'Bob lost his job, and *defaulted* on his mortgage payments'.

Deflation

A general sustained downward movement of prices for goods and services in an economy.

Direct Debit

A direct debit is set up by a bank account holder and allows the electronic transfer of money to a recipient, for example setting up regular payments for a cell phone bill.

Direct Deposit

Direct deposits allow a corporation, such as your employer, to electronically transfer money into your bank account, such as your paycheck.

. . .

Dividends

Regular payments that a company makes to its owners to share its profits. The board of directors of a company decides how much each share is worth and when and how often dividends are paid. Dividend stocks can give you a steady income, which can be especially helpful when prices increase.

Dow Jones Industrial Average (DJIA)

An index consisting of stock prices of 30 companies in various industries reflecting US economic activity.

Education Savings Account (ESA)

An Education Savings Account is a tax-advantaged savings account designed to help families save for education expenses. Contributions to an ESA are not tax-deductible, therefore the earnings within the account grow tax-free, and withdrawals for qualified educational expenses, such as tuition and books, are also tax-free. ESA funds can be used for elementary, secondary and higher education costs.

Equity

Equity = total assets - total debts. For example, if you buy a house worth $200,000 and borrow a $150,000 mortgage, your equity is $50,000.

Exchange-Traded Fund (ETF)

An Exchange-Traded Fund is a tradable investment fund that aims to replicate the performance of a specific index or asset class. ETFs provide diversification, liquidity and lower costs compared to traditional mutual funds and can be bought and sold on stock exchanges throughout the trading day.

. . .

Fair Market Value (FMV)

Fair Market Value is the price that something, such as a business or property, would sell in an open and competitive (as normal/fair as possible) market.

FICO Credit Score

The most widely used credit score. FICO stands for Fair Isaac Corp, the company that developed this credit evaluation system. FICO scores vary but generally range between 500 and 850. The higher the score, the more likely a borrower will repay loans/debts.

Foreclose

To take possession of a mortgaged property due to the borrower's failure to make mortgage payments.

Form 1040

Taxpayers use the standard Internal Revenue Service (IRS) form to file annual income tax returns.

Gross Income

The total amount earned before any adjustments are subtracted, for example, tax or student loans.

Health Insurance

Insurance that pays for medical and surgical expenses.

Hedge Fund

A pooled investment fund managed by professional portfolio managers, often using complex strategies and a wide range of financial instruments to seek higher returns for its investors.

Inflation

A general sustained upward movement of prices for goods and services in an economy.

Interest (Elementary)

An, often small, percentage of an account holders balance, paid into the account as a benefit from the bank for keeping your money with them. Reversely, interest is also an amount of money customers pay back to banks when they have taken out a loan. It is paid back *in addition* to the original amount borrowed.

Initial Public Offering (IPO)

An Initial Public Offering is a financial event in which a privately held company offers its shares to the public for the first time, allowing individuals and institutional investors to buy ownership stakes in the company.

Individual Retirement Account (IRA)

A retirement account that allows individuals to direct pretax or after-tax income, up to specific annual limits, toward investments that can appreciate.

Interest Rate

The percentage of the amount of a loan that is charged for taking out said loan. APR is an example of interest with a variable rate. Also, the percentage paid on a savings account.

Internal Revenue Service (IRS)

The Internal Revenue Service is the revenue service for the United States and enforces and administers US tax laws.

Levy

An amount of money, such as a tax, that has to be paid by a government or organization.

Liquidity

Liquidity refers to the ease with which an asset, or security, can be converted into ready cash without affecting its market price.

Loan

Money given to someone for a short time that must be paid back, usually with interest.

Market Economy

An economic system where buyers and sellers meet to exchange goods and services, and the buyers and sellers decide on price.

Medicare

A federal health care program that pays for certain medical and hospital costs for people aged 65 and older (and for some people under 65 and disabled); part of Social Security.

Mortgage

A loan for the purchase of real estate.

. . .

Mutual Fund

A company that pools investors' money and then issues shares to its investors.

NASDAQ

The National Association of Securities Dealers Automated Quotations system—a stock exchange where trades are made electronically.

Net Asset Value (NAV)

Net Asset Value is the value of all the assets held by a mutual fund, exchange-traded fund (ETF) or other investment vehicle minus any liabilities. It is typically calculated on a per-share basis. It represents the price at which investors buy or redeem fund shares. NAV reflects the underlying value of the fund's portfolio and is computed daily at the end of the trading day.

Net Pay

Gross pay minus deductions and taxes.

Payday Loan

A small, short-term loan intended to cover a borrower's expenses until his or her next payday. It may also be called a paycheck or payday advance.

Personal Identification Number (PIN)

A required code known only by the cardholder used to make transactions on their credit or debit card. The PIN is entered into a terminal (an ATM) and sent to an authorizing entity to verify the account.

. . .

Portfolio

A list or collection of financial assets that an individual or company holds.

Real Estate Investment Trust (REIT)

Businesses that own commercial real estate, such as office buildings, retail spaces, apartments and hotels, and pay investors from the rental income they receive.

Rent

A periodic payment made by a tenant to a landlord in exchange for the use and occupancy of a property or asset.

Retirement Plan 401(k)

A retirement plan sponsored by an employer that allows employees of a company to save and invest for their retirement on a tax-deferred basis. Employers may use 401(k) plans to distribute company stock to employees.

Return on Investment (ROI)

A way of measuring the effectiveness of an investment. ROI is calculated by the net gain (total earnings minus original investment) divided by the investment cost. For example, if you had $1200 from a $1000 investment, your net gain is $200, therefore your ROI is 20%.

Revolving Credit

A line of available credit, usually designed to be used repeatedly with a preapproved credit limit. The available credit decreases and increases as funds are borrowed and paid with interest.

· · ·

Risk/Reward Relationship

The idea that there is a direct relationship between the risk of the loss of principal and the expected rate of return. The higher the risk of loss of principal for an investment, the greater the potential reward. Conversely, the lower the risk of loss of principal for an investment, the lower the potential reward.

S&P 500

The S&P 500, short for Standard & Poor's 500, is a widely recognized stock market index in the United States. It measures the performance of 500 large, publicly traded companies listed on American stock exchanges. The index is designed to provide a snapshot of the overall health and performance of the US stock market by tracking the market capitalization of these selected companies across various sectors.

Security Deposit

Money paid by a tenant to a landlord that the landlord holds during the occupancy. It may be used to pay for any damage or unpaid rent when the lease ends or must otherwise return to the tenant. State laws dictate how soon it must be repaid after the lease ends.

Stagflation

The condition of relatively high inflation and relatively high unemployment occurring simultaneously.

Stock

A share of ownership in a company. Stocks are often traded publicly.

Tax Refund

Money owed to taxpayers when their total tax payments are greater than the total tax owed. Refunds are received from the government.

Term insurance

A policy provides coverage for a specific period, such as ten years. When the policy term ends, the insurance expires.

Uniform Gifts to Minors Act (UGMA)

A Uniform Gifts to Minors Act account is a custodial account established in the United States to hold and manage assets for a minor, typically a child. The account is set up and managed by an adult custodian, often a parent or guardian, who oversees the investments until the minor reaches the age of maturity, at which point the assets are transferred to the minor's control. UGMA accounts allow for various types of assets, such as cash, securities and real estate to be held and invested for the minor's benefit.

Uniform Transfers to Minors Act (UTMA)

A Uniform Transfers to Minors Act account is a custodial account in the United States that allows adults to gift assets to a minor, usually a child or grandchild. Like a UGMA account, a UTMA account allows for various types of assets, including cash, securities and real estate to be transferred to the minor. The appointed custodian manages the assets until the minor reaches the age of maturity, at which point the ownership of the assets is transferred to the minor and they gain control over the account. UTMA accounts provide a way to transfer assets to minors while receiving certain tax advantages.

Warranty

A guarantee to a consumer that promises a product or service will perform as intended.

Wire Transfer

A wire transfer is an electronic funds transfer that moves money from one account to another. It enables money to be transmitted securely without the need for cash exchange. Wire transfers are usually used for one-off payments. In contrast, direct deposits and debits are commonly automated and used for regular payments such as a salary or fixed bill.

REFERENCES

AABRS. (2023). Managing Small Business Finances. Retrieved from https://www.aabrs.com/managing-small-business-finances/

Annuity.org. (2023). Personal Finance. Retrieved from https://www.annuity.org/personal-finance

Bankrate. (2023). Passive Income Ideas. Retrieved from https://www.bankrate.com/investing/passive-income-ideas/

CareerAddict. (2022). How to Write a Student CV (With Examples). Retrieved from https://www.careeraddict.com/student-cv

CNBC. (2020). What Are Checking Accounts? Retrieved from https://www.cnbc.com/select/what-are-checking-accounts/

CollegeVine. (2023). 14 Awesome Internships for High School Students. Retrieved from https://blog.collegevine.com/14-awesome-internships-for-high-school-students/

Consumer Financial Protection Bureau. (n.d.). An Essential Guide to Building an Emergency Fund. Retrieved from https://www.consumerfinance.gov/an-essential-guide-to-building-an-emergency-fund/

Discover. (2023). 3 Reasons to Save More Money. Retrieved from https://www.discover.com/online-banking/banking-topics/3-reasons-to-save-more-money/?ICMPGN=OS-BK-HDSERCH

Endowus. (2021). Power of Compounding Interest. Retrieved from https://endowus.com/insights/power-of-compounding-interest

Experian. (2022). How to Set SMART Financial Goals. Retrieved from https://www.experian.com/blogs/ask-experian/how-to-set-smart-financial-goals/

Forbes Advisor. (2022). What Is Investing? Retrieved from https://www.forbes.com/advisor/investing/what-is-investing

Get Schooled. (2023). How to Start a Cover Letter for Teens. Retrieved from https://www.getschooled.com/article/5840-how-to-start-a-cover-letter-for-teens/

Good Financial Cents. (2023). Multiple Streams of Income: What Are They and Why You Need Them. Retrieved from https://www.goodfinancialcents.com/multiple-streams-of-income

ICICI Prudential Life Insurance. (n.d.). Importance of Savings. Retrieved from https://www.iciciprulife.com/protection-saving-plans/importance-of-savings.html

Indeed. (2023). Cover Letter for High School Student. Retrieved from https://au.indeed.com/career-advice/resumes-cover-letters/cover-letter-for-high-school-student

Indeed. (2023). How to Find a Job as a Teenager. Retrieved from https://www.indeed.com/career-advice/finding-a-job/how-to-find-job-as-teenager

Indeed. (2023). Interview Tips for Teens: How to Prepare and

Succeed. Retrieved from https://www.indeed.com/career-advice/inter viewing/interview-tips-for-teens

Indeed. (2023). Phone Interview Tips to Get You to the Next Round. Retrieved from https://www.indeed.com/career-advice/inter viewing/phone-interview-tips-to-get-you-to-the-next-round

Indeed. (2023). Top Online Jobs for Teens: Earning Money from Home. Retrieved from https://www.indeed.com/career-advice/find ing-a-job/top-online-jobs-for-teens

Investopedia. (2023). Bank Credit. Retrieved from https://www. investopedia.com/terms/b/bank-credit.asp

Investopedia. (2023). Checking Account. Retrieved from https:// www.investopedia.com/terms/c/checkingaccount.asp

Investopedia. (2023). Compound Interest. Retrieved from https:// www.investopedia.com/terms/c/compoundinterest.asp

Investopedia. (2022). Emergency Fund. Retrieved from https://www. investopedia.com/terms/e/emergency_fund.asp

Investopedia. (2021). Insurance Coverage. Retrieved from https:// www.investopedia.com/terms/i/insurance-coverage.asp

Investopedia. (2022). Investing. Retrieved from https://www.investope dia.com/terms/i/investing.asp

Investopedia. (2022). Real Estate Investing Guide. Retrieved from https://www.investopedia.com/mortgage/real-estate-investing-guide/

Investopedia. (2023). Risk/Reward Ratio. Retrieved from https:// www.investopedia.com/terms/r/riskrewardratio.asp

Investopedia. (2023). Savings Account. Retrieved from https://www. investopedia.com/terms/s/savingsaccount.asp

Investopedia. (2023). Taxes. Retrieved from https://investopedia.com/ terms/t/taxes.asp

Maryville University. (2023). Tax Planning Strategies. Retrieved from https://online.maryville.edu/blog/tax-planning-strategies/

MoneyHelper. (n.d.). Savings Accounts for Children. Retrieved from https://www.moneyhelper.org.uk/en/savings/types-of-savings/ savings-accounts-for-children

N26. (2022). The 50/30/20 Rule. Retrieved from https://n26.com/en- eu/blog/50-30-20-rule

Robbins Research International. (n.d.). Achieve Lasting Weight Loss with Delayed Gratification. Retrieved from https://www.tony robbins.com/achieve-lasting-weight-loss/delayed-gratification/

Rutgers, The State University of New Jersey, New Jersey Agricul- tural Experiment Station. (2009). Personal Finance: Making Money Work for You. Retrieved from https://njaes.rutgers.edu/sshw/ message/message.php?p=Finance&m=122

StandOut CV. (2023). CV Template for Teenagers. Retrieved from https://www.standout-cv.com/pages/cv-template-teenager

The Balance Money. (2022). Tips for Finding a Job for Teens. Retrieved from https://www.thebalancemoney.com/tips-for-finding-a- job-for-teens-2058651

The Economic Times. (2023). Credit. Retrieved from https://economic times.indiatimes.com/definition/credit

The Economic Times. (2023). Debt. Retrieved from https://economic times.indiatimes.com/definition/debt

The Motley Fool. (2023). Real Estate Investing Basics. Retrieved from https://www.fool.com/investing/stock-market/market-sectors/real-estate-investing/basics/

The Muse. (2021). Job Interview Tips for Teens. Retrieved from https://themuse.com/advice/job-interview-tips-for-teens

The Muse. (2023). Video Interview Tips: How to Ace a Virtual Interview. Retrieved from https://www.themuse.com/advice/video-interview-tips

Thinkific. (2023). Personal Branding Guide. Retrieved from https://thinkific.com/blog/personal-branding-guide/

United Way. (2020). 5 Benefits of Teen Volunteering. Retrieved from https://www.unitedwayhelps.org/blog/5-benefits-of-teen-volunteering

UpCounsel. (2023). Retrieved from https://www.upcounsel.com

Vanguard. (n.d.). Building an emergency fund. Retrieved from https://investor.vanguard.com/investor-resources-education/emergency-fund

Young and the Invested. (n.d.). Retrieved from https://youngandtheinvested.com

Flaticon. (n.d.). Coin Icon. Retrieved from https://www.flaticon.com/free-icon/coin_126191?term=dollar+sign&page=1&position=11&origin=tag&related_id=126191